RAILROADING in the WILD WEST

This long abandoned 1937 Chevrolet Coupe has only sage brush and creosote trees for company, that is if one ignores a very lengthy BNSF mixed manifest waiting 'in the hole' probably for an 'out of time' crew change. Heading the massive eastbound train are six units including two versions of the 'Heritage' paint scheme applied to the lead Dash 9-44CWs 968 and 4792, followed by a quartet of SD40-2s, led by BN liveried 7203 and 6362. The site is near Edwards Air Force Base, California where the NASA space shuttle sometimes landed. The Tehachapis can just be detected in the far distance.

RAILROADING
in the
WILD WEST

JOHN VAUGHAN

All photographs by the Author

A Photrack Production

3

First published 2011

ISBN 978-0-9522190-0-2

© John Vaughan 2011

Published by Photrack, P.O. Box 5338, Goring by Sea, Worthing, West Sussex, England, BN12 4DN

Printed in England by Ian Allan Printing Ltd, Hersham, Surrey, KT12 4RG

Front Cover: This wonderful wild western scene in the Californian Mojave desert, features westbound double stacks near Ivanpah in May 1996, just a few miles from the Nevada state line. A three locomotive lash-up comprising classic EMD SD40-2s is working hard on the long slog up Cima Hill while making its way to Los Angeles via Barstow. The consist comprises Union Pacific (UP) examples 3615 and 3322 and a single Chicago & North Western Transportation Company (CNW) machine 6896.

Back Cover: A delightful day is in prospect east of the Tehachapi Mountains, visible in the background. At 09.17 on 11 October 1998 a mixed manifest rolls off the hills and into Mojave behind Burlington Northern Santa Fe (BNSF) SD40u 6304, former Atchison Topeka & Santa Fe (ATSF) F45 cowl unit 5980, leased back to BNSF by Morrison Knudsen, and 'Warbonnet' C40-8W 871. The desert is blooming with the colour of the foreground flowers complementing the Santa Fe 'bluebonnet' livery of the lead locomotives.

Half title: Dawn has just broken in the Mojave 'sink' and the weak light from the misty early morning sun is illuminating the side of the double stacks and piggyback lorry trailers (or 'pigs' for short) comprising this westbound working. At 06.48 this 'before breakfast' shot shows BNSF 923 and 812 starting their climb over the Tehachapis, the C40-8Ws providing more than enough power for this rather short train. Beyond the distant road bridge the route divides, the former Southern Pacific (SP) line to Palmdale heading south and the old ATSF rails heading east to Barstow and beyond.

Title page: The spectacular Rainbow Canyon is located between Elgin and Caliente in Meadow Valley Wash country in the State of Nevada. Passing beneath the towering craggy rocks on 12 April 1997 is an eastbound train of empty coal hoppers returning to the Provo, Utah area headed by UP C36-7 9004, SP AC44CW 375 and a pair of UP SD60s 6066 and 6074.

4

CONTENTS

INTRODUCTION

This book is not about gunslingers, legendary lawmen, 'cowboys and Indians' or Hollywood's interpretation of the 'Wild West' through the acting efforts of Gary Cooper, John Wayne, Clint Eastwood, Gabby Hayes or Jack Elam, but a joyous celebration of trains running through some of the most magnificent scenery in the world. Mountains, forests, rivers, deserts and canyons plus a plethora of unforgettable National Parks infest the states of the Western USA attracting vast numbers of visitors from far and wide. This is 'something for everyone' country epitomised in California by Mount Whitney, the highest mountain in the Sierra Nevada range at 14,505ft, being just 76 miles distant from Badwater in Death Valley located a remarkable 282ft below sea level. Similarly it is hard to compare a cold wet day in the forests of the Cascade Mountains of Washington with the searing heat of a summer's day at Needles, California. The variety of the countryside, the climate and the trains that operate in the west is seemingly infinite.

WESTERN HISTORY
Native American history in the west can be traced back over ten thousand years. Early 16th century west coast seafaring explorers included Juan Cabrillo, Juan de Fuca, Francis Drake and Sebastian Cermenho. Having been established in Mexico for centuries settlers of Spanish origin were present in the west through their missions from 1769. Of particular note Captain George Cook in 1778 and Captain George Vancouver in 1792 explored the west coast of what became known as British Columbia. However modern history started in earnest with the pioneer trail blazers of the early 19th century and the great gold rush of the late 1840s and 1850s, when prospectors and speculators invaded the west in large numbers, especially the California Mother Lode country, in search of their fortunes. Few realised their ambitions and it is said that those selling picks, shovels and pans were the only ones to make a profit in the early years. With

During the mid-1980s the SP and ATSF railroads entered discussions about the possibility of a merger. Talks were encouraging with both companies seeing advantages at the prospect of a super railroad. So confident were the SP and ATSF that the merger would go ahead that they repainted large numbers of locomotives in the proposed red and yellow colour scheme, SP painting over 100 examples and ATSF 320 locomotives. The planned identity was to be SPSF and the lettering layout was arranged with this in mind. To the surprise of many, government authorities failed to authorise the merger and over time the painters were again at work deleting what had become know as 'Kodachrome' livery. Old stager SD9E 4377 was photographed at SP's Roseville yard as late as October 1995, still in merger livery.

burgeoning populations transport became increasingly important. It could take up to six months to make the arduous journey from the Mississippi River to the west coast by wagon train, six months to travel in dreadful conditions in small wooden sailing vessels from the east coast to San Francisco via the treacherous seas around Cape Horn, or almost the same amount of time to struggle across the Gulf of Mexico and negotiate the disease infested Isthmus of Panama, only to spend weeks awaiting a northbound sailing vessel. These early travellers suffered the rigours of travel coping with rugged terrain, bad weather, mud, dust and sand, bad water, poor food, temperature extremes, and justifiably hostile native tribes, with perhaps the 'Donner Party' producing the most dramatic story of the era. In the late autumn of 1846 and having chosen a new route, the Hastings cutoff, this wagon train failed by just days to cross the Sierra Nevada mountain range before the snows set-in. They ran out of food and temperatures were freezing. As the pioneers died from exposure and malnutrition some resorted to cannibalism in order to survive the entire winter. Of the 87 participants only 48 reached California in the Spring of 1847. In the early days the horse was most important in terms of personal transportation, small express companies delivered the mails to remote encampments and for longer distances the short lived Pony Express was born. All goods were transported by mules or horse drawn wagons, although in parts river navigation was used to advantage. Eventually the stage coach appeared with such names as Butterfield and Wells Fargo coming to the fore.

TRANSPORT HISTORY

Railroads had been established in the east by the 1830s and slowly but surely iron roads spread westward. However the great east to west transcontinental link by rail was not completed until 10 May 1869 when Leland Stanford drove the 'golden spike' into the last section of track at Promontory Point, Utah, linking the Union Pacific and Central Pacific Railroads. From that time it was

One of the most remarkable diesel locomotives ever built was the EMD DDA40X 'Centennial' class. Between 1969 and 1971 47 examples were built and all were fitted with wide FP45 driving cabs. With two EMD 645E3A 3,300hp diesel engines fitted to the 98ft 5in long 270 ton locomotives they were the longest and most powerful single units ever built in the US. They were geared for 90mph running, faster than the permitted speeds of some of their trailing loads, and incorporated modular electronic control systems, the precursor of the 'Dash-2' era. Every one of the impressive locomotives covered over two million miles before their intensive use took a toll in terms of maintenance costs. Most of the fleet were withdrawn by 1986 and the last in the year 2000 but 13 have been preserved. This view shows No 6946 at Portola, California. Note the eight wheeled trucks (bogies). No 6936 is in active retirement with UP in the 21st century.

possible to cross the continent in seven days, a remarkable technological achievement, with the efforts of the Chinese labourers in the Sierras being renowned. The route was not however seamless until 1872 and the honour of the first through 'continuous' rail route went to the Kansas Pacific Railroad in 1870 (later absorbed by the UP). The first trans-Canadian through route was completed in 1885. Over the decades the railway network spread throughout the west as both main lines and branch lines rapidly spawned, bringing with them telegraphic communications. In addition to passenger trains freight gradually became even more important and over the years every conceivable commodity was transported by rail, with dedicated tracks being provided for numerous industries, particularly logging and mineral extraction.

This was the age of steam when loads were light and speeds were slow but over time locomotive size and therefore power dramatically increased and payloads became considerably heavier and trains longer. From the turn of the 20th century the internal combustion engine started to affect the railways, not only in offering transport alternatives but also greater flexibility. With the mass manufacture of automobiles, trucks and buses came the creation of potential competition to the railways. However for long distance hauls the railroads remained supreme with for example the famous original 2,446 mile Route 66 from Chicago to Los Angeles not finally being paved throughout until 1938. Although there were earlier experiments, by the 1930s the internal combustion engine, particularly in diesel form, was being used in locomotives with the USA becoming world leaders in the manufacture of diesel traction units on railroads. Fleets of 'first generation' diesel locomotives were gradually delivered and although pockets of steam traction remained, by and large steam power was replaced by diesel during the 1950s. Following World War 2 the railroads of the USA and Canada again came under pressure by the development of air travel with aeroplanes covering the longer distances in hours rather than days.

Nearly all of the photographs within these pages pre-date such high-tech machinery as featured here. Absolutely brand new in this May 2005 shot at Nipton, California is UP 5464, a GE ES44AC 4,400hp GEVO 12-cylinder engined locomotive that was the successor of the GE Dash 9-44CW. Called C45ACCTE by UP, the locomotives have electronic fuel injection and low tier 2 emission standards (one might almost say 'fourth generation' machinery). UP have ordered over 500 of these locomotives to meet the message in their patriotic 'Building America' logo; flying the stars and stripes indeed.

This resulted in the decline of long distance passenger services on railroads throughout North America.

The road haulage industry also threatened the railroads with increasingly larger trucks travelling over quickly improving highways and a national road network that included multi-lane Interstate highways. Nevertheless for high tonnage long distance freight transportation the railroads were and still are supreme, especially since the development of bulk handling methods for containers and vehicle trailers. The delivery of 'second generation' diesel locomotives combined with railroad amalgamations on a spectacular scale increased railroad efficiency, albeit after the resolution of teething troubles, and with the Sage of Omaha, Warren Buffet, heavily investing in railroads during 2009 through his Berkshire Hathaway company, the business world clearly has every confidence that the railroads of the USA and Canada have a bright and profitable long term future. However in recent decades the major railroads have either closed or sold off many minor, secondary or duplicate lines as non-core businesses. Private companies have taken over some of them, making a living by handling a few cars per day as feeders to Class 1 railroads, and some are featured within these pages.

INSIDE PAGES

The history of specific aspects of American and Canadian railroads either by State, individual railway company, particular class of locomotive, type of topography or category of train, has been written about and photographed by learned authors and cameramen on numerous occasions and will not be repeated in detail here. While it is obviously not possible in such a vast geographical area and with a finite number of pages to include every main and branch line, railroad company, class of locomotive, and type of train, the carefully selected photographs putting the train in the landscape will hopefully provide the reader with an interesting cross section of images to be seen

One of the most unusual and under photographed railroads in the wild west is the Black Mesa & Lake Powell Railroad. The self contained electrified line has the sole purpose of conveying coal from a strip mine to the Navajo Power Plant near Page, Utah. Much of the track runs through a Native American reservation. The specially built single cab GE locomotives emerged from the factory between 1972 and 1976 and are designated E60C with an output of 6,000hp. In arid surroundings this trio were photographed at Black Mesa in August 1987. The fleet has since been augmented by some ex-Mexican National Railway examples.

along many of the rail routes in the 'Wild West'. Contained within these pages are illustrations of trains in action in the remarkable topography to be found in Arizona, California, Colorado, Idaho, Montana, Nevada, New Mexico, Oregon, Utah, Washington, Wyoming and British Columbia. The photographs also show the gradual changeover from 'second generation' diesel traction to the latest 'third generation' high powered high-tech locomotives, primarily from Electro-Motive Diesels (now Caterpillar and formerly Electro-Motive Division of General Motors) and General Electric stables. The products from other manufacturers such as the American Locomotive Company (ALCo) and Baldwin survive on secondary and

branch or 'short' lines and many of these are also featured. This armchair tour of trains in magnificent surroundings will hopefully provide bucket loads of nostalgia in bringing back memories of even recent scenes that cannot now be repeated and which have gone forever. The photographs within these pages have been mostly recorded in natural surroundings that constitute the 'Wild West', rather than towns or cities, although the 'wrong' end of many cities can be pretty 'wild'! Great patience has been required to secure many of these pictures, with only a couple of vaguely timed trains per day on some lines and even weekly trains on some of the branches. Please be aware that change is perpetual and this book's

geographical coverage so vast, some of the information about train workings, the status of routes, the liveries and particularly numbering of locomotives and the survival of buildings etc. may now be history. It would not be possible to revisit every site featured to check on the current status. Note also that railroad companies describe similar locomotives in different ways and variety in model designations can occur. The inclusion of maps would have been on such a small scale that not only would they have served no useful purpose but valuable pages would have taken up. In any event it would be an insult to the intelligence of our readers to spell-out where California is located in relation to Oregon or Nevada! Detailed railway

Those who indulge in railroad photography in the wild west need to be aware of a number of critters, some of which can be dangerous and on rare occasions lethal, especially to youngsters. Special care needs to be taken around desert plants and also under rocks. There are over 20 species of rattlesnake and this fellow, with rattle raised and vibrating, greeted the author lineside near Nipton, California. The Mojave rattlesnake is particularly venomous and if bitten it can affect the respiratory system. Never pick up a desert tortoise, a protected species, because they can urinate in shock and lose body fluids, which can be fatal to them. Scorpions are also best avoided!

maps are commercially available and therefore maps have been excluded.

PHOTOGRAPHY AND PRODUCTION

For the camera buffs, all of the images appearing within these pages were taken on 35mm FM2 and F301 Nikon film cameras using prime Nikkor lenses with a 35mm to 300mm range. Film emulsions are from the Kodak and Fuji companies and film speeds vary from 64-200asa. Processing has mostly been by the pleasant and competent staff of VPS Imaging at Goring by Sea, West Sussex, England. Technical preparation and detailed pre-publication design was by my old colleague Alan Butcher and another friend, Richard Cossey, gave the comprehensive manuscript the 'once-over' with his expert eye.

Production was by the Ian Allan Printing team at Hersham, Surrey, England. Their combined help is gratefully acknowledged. There is a mix of traditional and 'new approach' photography within these pages but in terms of shooting in perfect lighting or the ideal time of day the short term visitor is at a disadvantage compared with the local expert enthusiast. In any event in the western USA and Canada there is often no need to get clever photographically for the sake of it because normally the splendid scenery provides superb backgrounds, which combined with variable lighting conditions, time of year and weather often conspire to produce excellent pictorial images. I have enjoyed what seems over time to have been an

almost infinite variety of locomotives, trains and liveries while not having a special affinity with any particular railway. One major error was made over the decades and that was exposing only monochrome film for far too long and those black and white shots of Western Pacific 'F' units in action are likely to end their days in my personal photographic albums! If ever a geographical area lent itself to colour photography it is that covered within these pages.

THE AUTHOR

As an Englishman born in Vancouver, Canada during 1943, of English parents, with a Grandfather who worked on the Canadian Pacific Railway a century ago, and having lived in California for a couple of years in 1963/4, with over 30

Flash floods and desert washes are easily underestimated by the inexperienced and unwary. Every year over 130 people are killed in flash floods in the USA, normally by drowning and with over half being inside swept away road vehicles. Storms many miles away can dump millions of gallons of water onto distant hillsides, the deluge overwhelming rivers, creeks and washes and travelling at increasing speed, which catches-out campers and hikers. The author witnessed this scene at Paria, Utah in September 1999, the morning after a terrible flash flood gouged out the centre of the old film set ghost town. During 1976 Clint Eastwood stood at this remote spot while making the movie 'The Outlaw Josey Wales'.

vacation visits to the Western USA and Canada since the late 1970s, I feel at least partially qualified to produce this pictorial volume on the railroads of what is internationally known as the 'Wild West'. My first 'western' photograph, taken on a small child's plastic box camera, was of a trio of Canadian Pacific 'F' units at Revelstoke, British Columbia in August 1953, aged 10. However since 1979 thousands upon thousands of miles have been covered in pursuit of photographing trains in the western USA and Canada, in all seasons of the year and in all climatic conditions. Now in retirement and a 'pensioner' it has been my privilege to author 45 railway books in the UK during the past 45 years as well as writing scores of illustrated articles and editing a national railroad magazine for four years. However until now a volume such as this has been my last unrealised publishing ambition, an objective hereby achieved before complete retirement that is planned for 2012. Overall a common language shared by the United Kingdom, the USA and Canada is a natural bond between nations but for those 'over the pond' you will notice some 'English' spellings in some of the text and captions!

THE WEST IS STILL WILD

In retrospect I have been rather unwise and extremely lucky in my pursuit of trains in the magnificent American west. As a normally responsible adult I inexplicably ignored just about every public warning given out about travel in the wilderness, reflected in many of the these photographs. I implore readers not to take the chances that I have taken, with only scant attention being given to risk. Above all else never travel alone 'off the beaten track', as I have done on many occasions. At the age of 63 I unexpectedly suffered a heart attack and although I have (hopefully!) made a full recovery, if the event had happened on a desert hillside 25 miles from the nearest paved road rather than at home then I would certainly not be writing this text. Never travel off road in an unsuitable vehicle or without basic tools, such as a jack and shovel. As I found out to my cost it is so easy to get bogged down in a dry desert wash with the family saloon car sinking in the sand right up to the floor pan. After many

When motoring in the desert it is advisable not only to have a four wheel drive vehicle but also a shovel and matting, or even a winch. While trying to track and photograph the Arizona & California Railroad between Cadiz and Rice your author mistook a wash for a dirt road at what appeared to be a junction, despite travelling with a DeLorme atlas. The two wheel drive family saloon sank to its floor pan and single handed it was impossible to shift, despite the use of timbers. Being some 20 miles from the nearest paved road with zero population and 100F temperatures it was a scary moment. After what seemed an indeterminable period an ARZC four wheel drive high rail came to the rescue, saving me and the day. Off roading in such a vehicle is not recommended.

hundreds of miles of trouble free off-roading this happened to me over 20 miles from the nearest paved road and I was lucky to be rescued by a passing high rail four wheel drive vehicle. Also, remember that even a four wheel drive vehicle can become stuck in sand or mud. On another occasion an unseen rock holed the engine sump of my car. Never travel without a gallon of water because when I was stranded in a desert with the thermometer at over 100F I had just a pint of water in the car. If travelling off-road always carry a mobile 'phone. I have never had one while travelling in the USA, indeed in the early days there was no such thing, but now appreciate the value of such equipment. Always check the terrain and act with caution in remote areas, especially around old mines where deep shafts may not be capped-off. Everybody knows not to go rooting around in the undergrowth or to pick-up or dangle legs over large rocks as rattlesnakes do exist and a couple have confronted me (see photograph). Some scorpions can also deliver unpleasant and poisonous stings, especially the Arizona Bark Scorpion which can be fatal to children and pets. If encountered bears, buffalos and coyotes are best avoided.

Always use common sense and wear clothing suitable for the local conditions. I was on the paved highway in Byers Canyon, Colorado waiting to photograph a train after a heavy overnight rain storm when suddenly rocks started to fall from the cliff behind. Soon huge boulders the size of a family car started to fall and there is no doubt whatsoever that if one of these had fallen a little to the right or left I could have been killed or the hire car completely squashed! As if all this was not enough flash floods in arid desert regions are a real risk. I visited a movie set ghost town at Paria, Utah, about 40 miles east of Kanab, where many movies were made (the last being 'The Outlaw Josey Wales' with Clint Eastwood in 1976). Just hours before my visit to this isolated spot an overnight storm had produced a severe and dangerous flash flood that completely gouged-out the main street (see photograph). Many have been killed by

Another very real hazard in photographing trains can be the combination of topography and weather. Rock falls and landslips can occur in any mountainous region but especially after heavy rain where the subsoil beneath rocks is undermined. While innocently waiting for a train in Byers Canyon, Colorado in April 1995 and after heavy overnight rain, small rocks started to fall all around. Suddenly large rocks tumbled down the hillside and soon it was boulders. Just after snapping this scene the wheels of the hire car were spinning as your author beat his retreat. To have a rock of this size land on your head or the car could be lethal. Railroading in the west can indeed be wild!

flash floods, such as the tragedy in Antelope Canyon near Page, Arizona on 12 August 1997 when a wall of water killed 12 hikers. Throughout the USA an average of 133 people are killed every year by flash floods. Remember, it does not have to be raining at the location you are in for a flash flood to occur. These are real stories and it really is best to avoid risk just in order to get that 'mastershot'. Another warning applies to chasing trains for a second or third shot where the obsession of catching the train can lead to unintentionally exceeding local speed limits which can often be hard to determine. I have been stopped only twice by 'the law' but possibly because of being a visitor with an English accent I have 'got-off' with a verbal warning rather than a costly ticket, but don't assume you will share such good fortune!

CONCLUSION

On the whole the western American tourist scene of chain motels, which are clean and offer excellent value for money, is hard to beat. Similarly there always seems to be a choice of diners, drive-ins and restaurants available that are hygienic and good value for money. Hire cars with an unlimited mileage option are reasonably priced, although insurance extras can be high. Conditions of hire always stipulate no

off-roading and travels over the border to Mexico are an absolute 'no-no'! Over the years the price of a gallon of gasoline (petrol) has trebled from under $1 to over $3, with the US gallon being only four fifths of the British Imperial gallon. However even with distances between locations being much greater than the UK the cost of motoring is low compared with European standards, especially if costs are shared. The majority of American enthusiasts have radio scanners which enable them to listen in to communications between train crews, dispatchers and track gangs, giving notice of an approaching train (or not). I have never bothered with this facility, not wanting to lose the thrill of sighting a distant headlight. However I once waited seven hours for a train not knowing there was an engineer's possession on the line!

My travels in western North America have given me many hundreds of hours of immense pleasure and it is my wish, through the medium of this book, that you share my enjoyment. If you have never visited the wild west I hope the illustrations herein encourage you to make the effort to seek out some of these locations. You will not be disappointed. Having already dedicated past books to close family and friends I dedicate this book to all of the cameramen of the USA, Canada and

England, sadly too numerous to mention, who have chosen to pursue the stunning railway scene of the 'Wild West' and to all of the enthusiasts and railway modellers who find this unique part of the world so fascinating.

John Vaughan
Goring by Sea
Sussex, England

This view shows one of the dangers of lineside photography that can be found in some of the more remote parts of Nevada. This is one of many mines with uncapped shafts, although in this case rusty winding gear provides a clue to abandoned mining activity. These shafts are often several hundred feet deep and it can sometimes take 10 seconds for a thrown rock to reach the bottom of a shaft. Such sites are best avoided.

TEHACHAPI

Many say that the 69 miles of track between Bakersfield and Mojave in California over the Tehachapi Mountains, including the famous Tehachapi Loop, provides the finest stretch of mountain railroading in the world. In terms of moving large tonnages over a challenging terrain the assessment is probably correct. The line was largely built by Chinese labourers and was opened in 1876. The ruling gradient from Bakersfield to the 4,030ft summit at Tehachapi depot is 2.2 per cent, about 1 in 45. The surrounding mountains are almost twice that height. Thundering through the narrows in Caliente Canyon are eastbound double stacks powered by an impressive trio of powerful BNSF Dash 9-44CW locomotives, 984, 1034 and 4806. It was not until 1994 that the tunnels on the Tehachapi route were re-engineered to accommodate double stacks.

Right: They say that the early bird catches the worm, in this case a long timber train that had travelled all the way from the Pacific Northwest via Dunsmuir, Roseville and the Central Valley. With the very early morning light just brushing the oak studded hills and glinting dramatically off the locomotive's sides, the grade between Caliente and Tunnel #1 is obvious even with a standard camera lens. Ex-BN SD40-2s 6841, 6715 and 7059 are boosted by ATSF Dash 8-40CW 860. During 1983 heavy rains swelled the local Caliente, Tehachapi and Cache Creeks resulting in severe floods and washouts west of Caliente, closing the line for some time. The crew will be hoping for an uninterrupted run with their eastbound train that is briefly running westbound!

Left: The local photographer always has the advantage over the visitor in knowing precisely when lighting conditions at specific locations at certain times of the day and year are going to be dramatic. At 17.40 on 26 March 1996 the setting sun just 'peeps' down the Caliente Narrows providing strong back lighting to any emerging eastbound. With the aid of a telephoto lens the shot was taken from a public road just below Tunnel #1, the exhaust notes from the EMD SD45s echoing off the mountainsides and filling the valley with sound. ATSF SD45-2 5867 leads Dash 9-44CW 610, SD45 5325 and GP60M 124 and soon the consist will be travelling in darkness as they grind their way through the mountains to Mojave and on to Barstow.

There is no doubt that in terms of sheer weight the most impressive train to be lifted over the Tehachapis was the Bakersfield to Delores (Los Angeles) fuel tanks colloquially known as 'The Cans', train symbol BKDOU. The statistics were remarkable with 1.8 million gallons of fuel being conveyed in 78 large GATX tank cars grossing to 10,334 tons. At 3hp per ton the mechanical department had to ensure that 30,000hp of motive power was available, often with six locomotives on the point and four more cut-in about two thirds of the way down the train. The train ran from 1983 until 1997 when a new pipeline and loading terminal came into service at Mojave. With an explosion of sound and clouds of exhaust the head end power of this working shake the foundations of the former depot at Bealville, elevation 1,688ft. During 1952 a severe earthquake in the area measuring 7.5 on the Richter scale closed the line for 26 days and resulted in the old Tunnel #4 being abandoned and bypassed.

Here we see the 'Cans' again but this time negotiating the famous Tehachapi Loop on 9 March 1995. This remarkable head end consist is the most varied array of liveries that the author has ever encountered on a single train. Extreme centre right is Tunnel #9, which the train has just negotiated on its long climb from Bakersfield. The longest trains actually loop themselves at this location. Typically grubby SP tunnel motor SD40T-2 8299 leads CSX B36-7 5901, Conrail SD60M 5504, UP SD40B-2 B4255, Electro Motive GP60 demonstrator EMD 7, and SP Speedletter liveried SD45T-2 9400. Four swing helpers were assisting further back in the consist; DRGW 5380, SP 8319, SSW Cotton Belt 8373 and SP 8283! Overviews of the loop and Walong can be had from public roads and footpaths in the area. A roadside plaque commemorates this significant engineering achievement. There have been many books published about this railroad but Steve Schmollinger's 'Tehachapi – Railroading on a Desert Mountain' and 'Desert Railroading' are recommended, as well as Anthony Guppy's 'Thunder in the Mountains' on blurb.com.

Right: Having been a vibrant green in the Spring the California hills are now turning gold, as seen in the early autumn sunshine above the 370ft long Tunnel #10, east of the Tehachapi Loop. At 08.05 on 4 October 1998 a traditional mixed manifest freight with yellow and blue locomotives and seemingly endless box cars snake their way onwards towards the summit. Behind Dash 8-40B 7440 are F45u 6976, C30-7 8108, SD45u 5398, SD45-2 (cabless) 7505 and SD40-2 6754. Several of the units are former Santa Fe machines that have been leased back to BNSF and some will be costed on a 'power by the hour' basis. The last locomotive is passing the site of the old Tunnel #11, which was daylighted in 1943.

Selecting photographs for inclusion in this book from a large Tehachapi collection was extremely difficult. However this picture of 'The Cans' powering the last few yards towards the summit at Tehachapi depot in the very last moments of daylight on 27 March 1996 could not be resisted. Within seconds the setting sun would disappear behind the looming mountains. On this occasion eight locomotives were sufficient for the load, their numbers being SP 8283/8208/8696/8623, with swing helpers in the form of DRGW 5506/5514/5509/5505. Between 1880 and 2007 the population of Tehachapi grew from 255 to 12,077 with a total current catchment area of over 35,000. Residents would rather enjoy a refreshing climate and (for some) a long commute than live at the southern end of the hot Central Valley.

Strangers to California have romantic visions of permanent sunshine but particularly in the mountain regions low cloud and heavy rain can linger in the hills and summer storms can, seemingly, appear from nowhere. It is still winter in the Tehachapis as a double stack hotshot emerges from Tunnel #3 at Bealville in the most atrocious conditions on 5 March 1995. This is no time for fair weather photographers as ATSF widecabs 821/698/832/692/143 make their way west in full dynamic mode as a train load of several thousand tons, a steep down gradient and wet rails make for an unenviable combination. Although only single track at this point up to 36 freight trains per day can traverse the route giving the dispatchers quite a pathing headache on occasions.

Living nearly 6,000 miles from Mojave and being able to holiday only once or twice per year there is no time to be wasted as this 06.05 photograph demonstrates. Passing aloofly by with a westbound ATSF TOFC train (trailers on flat cars) is GP60M 106, supported by classmate 104, Dash 8-40BW 569 and two other locomotives. Although B-B locomotives such as this lead trio were capable racehorses on certain routes they were not generally favoured on the hill because with 3,800hp delivered through only four wheeled trucks they were prone to slipping. In sidings on the right is rebuilt SP SD45 7399, which in 1996 still sported the Kodachrome livery of the aborted mid-1980s ATSF/SP merger. Sometimes known as 'flares' the SP rebuilt a total of 133 SD45s as SD40-2Ms. The original 20 cylinder 3,600hp locomotive was an impressive but thirsty machine, referred to in some circles as 'hustle muscle'. Some were later down-rated to 3,200hp. In the background are some SP SD40T-2 and SD45T-2 tunnel motors including Nos 8258 and 9359.

Right: Proctor Lake near Monolith on the eastern side of Tehachapi is normally a dry lake but heavy winter rains in 1997/98 resulted in a recreation of times past. A BNSF four unit TOFC train heads west as evaporating low cloud has minutes to live. The nearby Monolith Cement Works was constructed in 1908 to provide cement for the Owens Valley to Los Angeles aqueduct, which was completed in 1913. It is now owned by Lehigh Southwest Cement. The hills nearby are covered with 5,000 power generating windmills, a figure exceeded only by Altamont Pass in Northern California. A new Los Angeles to San Francisco high speed railway line with an envisaged three hour journey time is planned to traverse the Tehachapi route but first somebody must stump-up over $10bn!

CABS and 'BOs

Right: In old movies it was not uncommon for travellers or 'Hobos' to hop a freight car for a free ride to the next town. A definition of hobo is a migratory worker or homeless vagabond, without sinister connotations. The hobo was often penniless and looking for work whereas a tramp was often a beggar who had no intention of working. Their numbers reached a peak after the American Civil War and during the great depression of the late 1920s and early 1930s. Nowadays trains are harder to ride, there are fewer box cars and freight trains travel much faster than hitherto. Nevertheless your intrepid photographer snapped these three 'Bos (and a dog!) at Cienega Creek, Arizona on the SP (now UP) Sunset Route in 1996. The train was headed by SP No 8256 but where would it next stop?

Below: It seems that not so long ago every north American freight train had a caboose attached. The official definition of a caboose is "a railroad car with accommodation for the train crew, normally the last car on a freight train". Unfortunately with the introduction of hot box detectors, electronic end of train devices (EOT or FREDs) and with the universal use of roller bearings on freight car trucks, the caboose gradually became redundant, finally disappearing from Class 1 roads in the 1980s, except where back-up moves have to be made. Some operational examples survive on short lines while many others are perched on plinths in children's playgrounds. SP 4759 is about to disappear into Tunnel #9 on the Tehachapi Loop at the end of a maintenance of way (civil engineer's) train in 1996.

Below right: 'Railroading in the Wild West' mainly features 'second generation' diesel traction with the gradual appearances of modern high-tech, high adhesion, low emission, 'third generation' machinery. The 'first generation' diesels had mostly been withdrawn by the start of the timescale covered within these pages but many still exist at industrial locations, on short lines, or are preserved at various tourist lines and museums. One example is Santa Fe F7A 347C and F3B 347B, both of 1949, seen here at the California State Railroad Museum at Sacramento. All of the State transport museums are well worth a visit, while privately owned installations, such as the Western Pacific Railroad Museum at Portola, California are also recommended.

Originally built in 1962/63 this number group of ATSF GP30s were rebuilt between 1978 and 1984, with a 16-cylinder 2,250hp specification and designated GP30u. The baseball capped engineer (driver) of BNSF No 2445 (formerly 2745) is testing his skills as he couples up to loads at the lumber company at Chinese Camp on the Sierra Railway, which runs eastward from Oakdale, California (see pages 82/83). The locomotive was on loan to the short line operator due to a motive power shortage. It was great to see the veteran still at work in 1999.

Below: In close-up the vast size of most locomotive cabs becomes apparent, dwarfing the average family car. The cab of BN GP38-2 2278 is seen in workaday condition at Easton on the Stampede Pass route across the Cascade mountain range in the State of Washington on 10 September 1997. The stencilled Burlington Northern name, the 'stars and stripes' and, lower right, the underframe bell are of interest. In company with GP38 2180 the pair were busy with an engineer's works train. Having arrived for a days photography the author was greeted with the news that there would be no trains running until 17.30 hours. The old Northern Pacific line dates back to 1888 and has always been plagued by washouts. It was closed in 1983 but reopened after rebuilding in the 1995/97 period. The tunnels on the line are too low for double stacks and auto racks and with only a handful of trains using the route each day plus a general recession from 2008 it was again mothballed in 2009.

Below: This typical US truck stop scene shows the cabs of nine colourful rigs at the now demolished Nevada Landing hotel/casino at Jean, Nevada. Truckers, the main rivals of the railroads, have a unique culture, which has been promoted by such movies as 1970 'Convoy' starring Kris Kristofferson and Ernest Borgnine. For the railfan trailers on flat cars has to be the most quietly satisfying sight!

SALT LAKE to ELKO

This location is now the nearest operational railway line to the famous Promontory Point, where the first transcontinental rail route was completed at the 'Golden Spike' ceremony in 1869. The original line was tightly curved and steeply graded and between 1902 to 1904 a massive trestle was built across part of the Great Salt Lake as part of an avoiding line. This new rail route from Ogden to Lucin became known as the Lucin Cut-off and was 43 miles shorter than the original route. The wooden trestle was replaced by a parallel causeway in the 1950s and the original wood was eventually reclaimed and reused. With dried salt in the foreground, the lake behind and snow covered distant mountains, these triple deck car carriers are hauled westward in April 1997 by UP C40-8s 9127 and 9168, which are sandwiching a filthy SP SD45T-2 tunnel motor.

There is a storm raging in the Ogden to Salt Lake City area as the weather backs up against the Wasatch Mountains. Fleeing the rain, thunder and lightning on the causeway across part of the Great Salt Lake are a trio of CNW C44-9s, 8619, 8635 and 8721 with a short westbound train of TOFC pigs. In taking over CNW in 1995 UP benefitted by inheriting some modern recently procured motive power that was immediately put to use far beyond the former CNW boundaries. Some of the CNW locomotives still survive in their original livery in late 2010. The first UP piggyback train trials took place way back in 1954.

Crossing the border from Utah to Nevada one of the first significant railroad features encountered on the 'southern' UP route is the Arnold Loop. The loop assists trains to climb from the Pilot Valley and over the Trona Mountain Range to the Goshute Valley, before crossing in succession the Pequop Mountains, Independence Valley, Independence Mountains and the formidable Humboldt Range. The loop was completed in 1914 avoiding the steeply graded original line. Brilliant engineering ensured that the gradient around the loop was a modest and consistent 1 per cent. A pair of UP 4,300hp SD90MACs, 8103 (leading) and 8010 (trailing), have SP AC44CW 198 for support on 19 April 1997. Beware of off-roading in this rugged soft sand area.

West of Wells both the former Western Pacific (WP) and SP (originally the Central Pacific) routes across northern Nevada ran broadly parallel, following the course of the Humboldt River as far as Winnemucca. For many years there was operational cooperation between the railroads whereby eastbound trains used the WP route and westbounds the SP line but with the UP taking over firstly the WP and secondly the SP both lines are now in their hands. West of the town of Elko the lines travel through Carlin and Palisade Canyons both popular with photographers. However between the two canyons stands a few remains of the old mining town of Palisade. In this view from the old pioneer cemetery an eastbound train emerges from the 1,060ft Tunnel #39 headed by SP AC44CW 263, UP SD40-2 3758, UP C44/60AC 7045 with some inspection doors missing, and SP AC44CW 256. The long abandoned 3ft gauge Eureka & Palisade Railroad once connected Palisade to various mills and mines to the south.

There are still traces of snow on the distant 7,522ft Sherman Peak in the Adobe Range. In the last vestiges of daylight at 17.46 on 18 April 1997 an eastbound merchandise runs along the WP/UP track near Deeth, a few miles east of Elko, behind UP SD40-2 3960, SP SD45T-2 5351 and SP SD45R 7504. The SP had 357 SD45s and while they performed well they eventually suffered crankshaft failures, over-stressed turbochargers and high fuel consumption. The first WP passenger train ran through here in 1910. A wealthy businessman had given the railway $10,000 to locate a roundhouse and repair shops at Elko and the company subsequently employed 170 local staff.

STREET RUNNING

The old Tidewater Southern Railway was, for most of its life, a subsidiary of WP. It was in the main an interurban railroad running electric car services between Stockton and Modesto via Escalon from 1913, with extended lines to Turlock and Hilmar. It succumbed to road competition, closing to passengers in 1932. Freight continued to be hauled throughout the decades and in 1986 UP took over the WP, including the Tidewater line. One of the great sights in the fruit and vegetable growing Central Valley was the daily Tidewater freight running down 9th Street in the heart of Modesto, seen here with UP GP40 667 and GP15-1 1598 on 28 June 1994. This route was abandoned in 2001 when trains were diverted via the old SP main line.

The Class 3 short line Central California Traction Company was incorporated on 7 August 1905. This was also an electrified interurban line that opened between Stockton and Lodi in 1907 and onwards to Sacramento in 1910. As with the Tidewater line, passenger services ceased, but in 1933 and in 1936 the Interstate Commerce Commission were arbitrators in bringing the CCTC into shared ownership between the WP, ATSF and SP. The company now operates in the Port of Stockton, the third largest port in California, and between Stockton and Lodi, the line to Sacramento being closed in August 1998. The company has interchange arrangements with BNSF, UP and STE in Stockton. Here CCT GP18 1790 rumbles through the residential streets of Stockton while working away from the BNSF's Mormon Yard.

Left: This view perfectly illustrates the need for a caboose on the Central California Traction network. Having completed its switching operations in the town of Lodi No 1790 propels its four box cars and the caboose past the local barber's shop on East Lodi Avenue in 1994. On reaching the yard at the eastern end of town the locomotive will either run round its train, collect any other cars and return to Stockton, or (until closed) continue to Sacramento. The brakemen keep a sharp lookout for recalcitrant motorists.

In many towns and cities in the western USA railroad tracks share the local streets with road vehicles. Although there are some notable exceptions, such as Jack London Square in Oakland, the tracks serve mainly industrial installations, rather than being part of a through route. Such an example can be found at Tracy, California where seasonal sugar beet traffic is delivered by rail to the refinery owned by Holly Sugar. Some of the beet comes from distant locations including Mexico. Having just arrived from Lathrop, St Louis South Western (SSW) SP GP60 9632 and Cotton belt/SP GP40-2 7619 trundle towards the SP (now UP) main line on 3 October 1995. The SP had 195 GP60s, 95 of which were lettered for the wholly owned SSW subsidiary, acquired way back in 1932. The Cotton belt identity was retained until 1992.

U.P. in UTAH

The small town of Lynndyl with a population of just 134 is located in northern Utah on the edge of the Sevier Desert. To the east of the town are the Sand Pitch Mountains, which are part of the Wasatch Range. Nearby is the vast Inter Mountain Power Project, which has a dedicated railway spur, and to the north the junction where the Leamington Cut-off to Provo diverges from the 1905 Los Angeles and Salt Lake route. Winter will soon be over, the snow will melt and the engineer will soon be able to dispose of his heavy lumber jacket. UP SD60M 6341 and C40-8 9317 will soon have their 110-car load heading south. Note the bullet holes in the adjacent signs, not an unusual occurrence in the wild west!

Echo Canyon lies south east of Ogden and north east of Salt Lake City. The road through the canyon was part of the Mormon Trail. The canyon is known for its colourful rock cliffs still with a lingering trace of snow on the top. At the small town of Echo at the foot of the canyon there was once a Pony Express station, a series of their riders travelling the 1,860 miles from St Joseph, Missouri to San Francisco in 10 days! A stage coach would take more than twice that time. In the days of steam there was a helper station at Echo. Climbing towards the summit with a container train on 27 April 1997 are UP SD60M 6186, LMS lease fleet GE C40-8W 709, SP ex-DRGW SD50 5504 with UP SD60M 6160 trailing. The Rio Grande purchased 17 SD50s in 1985 but they were not a great success.

The track through Echo and Weber Canyons at the northern end of the Wasatch Mountains dates back to 1869. It is a busy route with between 25 and 40 freight trains traversing the rails in a typical 24 hour period. It is now freight only as the last Amtrak passenger train from Chicago to Portland operated over this part of the route in 1997. From Ogden to Echo summit the line climbs over 2,500ft but the climb up the Wasatch grade is a modest 1.14 per cent. Until 1905, following a number of line deviations, Morgan station (seen here) was known as Weber. The last freight agent departed from this scene in 1985 and by April 1997 the old depot had gradually become more derelict. On the bleakest day imaginable the head end locomotive lighting brightened up the scene as UP SD60Ms 6169 and 6223 exited Weber Canyon and headed west past the dilapidated station buildings with a train of auto racks.

COLUMBIA RIVER

The mighty Columbia River is a spectacle to behold. Rising in the Rocky Mountains in British Columbia the river is 1,243 miles long and is the longest in the north west region. The largest of its many tributaries is the Snake River. The main section of river has 14 hydro-electric dams, more than any other US river, a situation enhanced by its steep average 2.16ft per mile drop that enhances the flow rate. It is one of only two rivers that breaches the Cascade range of mountains and for its final 309 miles it also marks the border between Oregon and Washington, which became States in 1859 and 1889 respectively. This 1911 railway bridge spans the Columbia River near Wishram, which links today's UP and BNSF. Seen in soft late afternoon lighting on a still day this BNSF train has worked along the Oregon Trunk 'Inside Gateway' from Bend, Oregon behind a trio of BN SD40-2s, 6836/8051/7835, and a Kansas City Southern SD60 753. KCS is now the smallest and second oldest Class 1 railroad.

The scenery along the Columbia River is varied and in places awesome, ranging from waterfalls and deep forests to desert bluffs. The route along the river was discovered in recent history terms by Lewis and Clark during their 1805 expedition and this opened up the area through what became known as the 'Oregon Trail'. The first railroad in the area dates back to 1851 when small wooden platform cars pulled by donkeys provided portage around non-navigable sections of the river. With the mountains in the Mount Hood area providing a fearsome looking backdrop an eastbound mixed manifest passes Wyerth at 09.57 on 12 September 1997 behind UP SD40-2 3449, MPI SD40M-2 leaser 9006 and UP C40-8 9335.

The first railway line to be built through the Columbia River Gorge was way back in 1883 but it was March 1908 when the Northern Pacific/Great Northern line was built, opening throughout from Spokane to Portland in 1909. Prior to the dams being constructed the Oregon Steam Navigation Company used part of the river for both passengers and freight. The dams adversely affected the flow of fish, particularly salmon and steelheads, to their natural spawning grounds but some bypass 'fish ladders' have now been provided. It is 08.45 in the morning and the mighty Columbia River never looked better as nearly new Heritage 1 liveried BNSF Dash 9-44CW 1069 double heads BN liveried SD40-2 7064 east of the John Day Dam with a container train destined for Pasco and beyond.

The basalt cliffs towards the eastern end of this part of the Columbia River Gorge are spectacular. This view looking east shows the south shore UP line, which parallels Interstate Highway 84. The first paved highway through the gorge was not completed until 1922 but it is now a major artery for road traffic. Dwarfed by the surroundings this westbound intermodal is nearing Philippi Canyon Road at 15.51 on 10 September 1997 headed by CNW liveried C44-9W 8705 (now UP 9809), supported by UP SD40-2 3971. A number of UP SD40s were re-geared for high speed intermodal services and these became SD40-2H or 'fast forties'.

On rare occasions lady luck is on the side of the railway photographer. Such was the case on this day when the author captured on film a Columbia River Gorge 'race' between westbound UP pigs in the foreground and westbound BNSF double stacks on the north side of the river. UP has approximately 8,700 locomotives on its roster and BNSF has a marginally more conservative 6,400. Ex-CNW SD50 5090 heads a brace of CNW C44-9Ws 8664 and 8648 (now UP 9768 and 9752). Showing the benefit of carrying binoculars, in the far distance BNSF Dash 9-44CW 1039 leads BN liveried SD40-2 8102 and SD40-2B 7501, the latter being a cabless rebuild of a wrecked unit. Again the photograph was taken from Philippi Canyon Road.

FEATHER RIVER ROUTE

Although there are of course hundreds if not thousands of great 'photspots' in the wild west, over the years a few dozen have become classics. One of these has to be the view from Highway 70 above the North Fork of the Feather River at Pulga, seen here. This part of the canyon is overlooked by such notable edifices as Flea Mountain and Bachelor Point. The 8 October 1995 was a beautiful day in Butte County, California as westbound double stacks threaded the canyon behind UP SD60M 6336, CNW liveried C40-8 8565 and UP SD60 6045. For most of its length the beautifully engineered line rises at a modest 1 per cent, half the gradient of the more southerly Donner Pass route over the Sierras.

Right: Over the years one of the joys of observing and photographing freight trains has been reading the logos and motifs of diverse and sometimes obscure railroad companies, many of which are now 'fallen flags'. This delightful Western Pacific 'Feather River Route' box car was photographed at Lodi, California in 1994 relegated to MoW service – notice the roof walk and grease axle boxes now prohibited in revenue earning service.

The Feather River Canyon is the most wonderful stretch of railway line with many memorable vistas. This section of track east of Belden is known as Serpentine Canyon, the name reflecting the curvature of the track. Many of the tunnels on this part of the route, including the delightfully named 'Honeymoon Tunnels', are cut through solid rock. In the mid-1980s the tunnels were enlarged to accommodate double stack container trains. A 57-car westbound grain train is seen near Rich Bar (a name left over from the gold rush days) powered by a trio of the evergreen UP SD40-2s, 3341/3298/3667 and GP40 682 in September 1994.

From 188ft at Oroville, California the Feather River Route climbs to 3,260ft at Keddie and 4,834ft at Portola before reaching the summit at Beckwourth Pass. The air is fresh in Plumas County at around the 4,000ft mark where the impressive Clio Viaduct, is located. Crossing the structure at 11.20 on 10 October 1995 in typical Plumas National Forest surroundings is an eastbound consist of auto racks headed by UP SD60M 6356, CNW SD60 8029 and, desperately in need of a repaint, a tired looking UP SD40-2 No 3463. There will be a crew change at Portola.

Right: The glorious Clio Viaduct is seen from an elevated viewpoint in the autumn sunshine on a lovely October day. Surrounded by conifers the viaduct is located at the southern end of the Mohawk Valley, with the small town of Clio and the Middle Fork of the Feather River both located nearby. The structure is 176ft from the ground and over 1,000ft long. This amply powered eastbound TOFC hotshot, containing a large number of orange coloured trailers belonging to the Schneider company, will still be climbing at this stage of its crossing of the Sierra Nevada mountain range. 'Lightning Strike' cab ends give a clue to the origins of the motive power; ex-CNW C44-9Ws 8682 and 8640, with less illustrious UP SD60M 6344 sandwiched between the two of them but making a 3,800hp contribution nonetheless.

Another classic photographic vantage point on the Feather River Route is Keddie Wye. The WP built the main line between 1906 and 1909 as part of their Oakland to Salt Lake City route. The single track 'Highline' seen here on the left was a later addition. It connected to the 'Inside gateway' route at Bieber, California. The viaduct and the nearby small town is named after Arthur W Keddie, the Scottish surveyor of the line in the early 20th century. In later Heritage 2 livery BNSF heavy metal in the shape of three BNSF C44-9Ws, 5330/4788/5142, roll off the former WP line in May 2007. The BNSF have running rights over the Feather River Route and traffic has been increasing in recent years. Gradually the rapidly growing conifers are obliterating the view for railway photographers.

On the eastern side of the Sierra mountain range annual rainfall levels are considerably lower due to the rain shadow effect and here the tree population rapidly thins out, giving the opportunity of wider vistas for train viewing. Having ended its long trek across northern Nevada westbound double stacks are seen approaching Reno Junction, California behind a colourful array of motive power, including UP SD70M 4886, FURX (First Union Rail Corporation) 8122, UP SD40-2 3176 and FURX No 8105. The origins of the SD40-2 leasers is obvious from their BN and BNSF paint schemes. The train will soon be passing the mothballed track to Reno, Nevada before plunging into the 6,002ft Tunnel #37 at Beckwourth Pass.

Left: The author has impishly positioned this photograph of Reno Junction, Wyoming to immediately follow that of Reno Junction, California. However the topography and the railroad scene could not be more different. From the visitor's perspective the scale of the Powder River Basin is almost impossible to grasp. The basin is 200 miles long on a north/south axis and 120 miles wide from east to west. It supplies 40 per cent of all of the mined coal in the USA and is the third largest source of natural gas. In 2007 gross coal output was 436m tons! In this impressive scene a truly massive coal train heads south on the main line powered by a pair of UP SD9043ACs, 8272 and 8242, and C44AC 6838. No 8242 was severely damaged on 9 August 2000 at Springfield, Colorado while working C-CQEYI-08 Cochise, Arizona to Energy, Colorado but was rebuilt in April 2001. Rolling off the spur from Black Thunder and Jacobs Ranch mines is another load with UP SD9043AC 8126 and SP liveried AC44CW 279 providing the horses.

There aren't too many trees in these high and windswept Wyoming hills! Gliding through the austere landscape at milepost 107 with the inevitable aluminium coal hoppers are UP AC4400CW 7128 and SP AC44CW 219. The tracks in the Powder River Basin have no great age with most being built between 1972 and 1979. The feeding corridors were all upgraded and widened in the 1990s because the 1990 Clean Air Act made the 'clean' Wyoming coal more attractive compared with dirtier West Virginian and Appalachian coal, resulting in more trains. In 2006 BNSF and UP announced a further $100m investment to provide three track capacity, with four track enlargement on steeply graded sections. There is currently talk of 200 car, 32,500 ton trains, being hauled by five modern high powered locomotives, although the 2008/2010 recession has seen coal loads drop by 15 per cent.

Transporting coal accounts for 20 per cent of both UP and BNSF income and it is therefore bad news that notwithstanding the 'green' movement and global warming theories most of the mines in the Powder River Basin have a projected life span of only about 20 years. The area is accessed from both a northerly direction near Gillette and a southerly direction south of Bill. Curving towards the northern 'exit' is this BNSF consist comprising a trio of SD70MACs, including 9776 in white and Grinstein green livery, and Heritage liveried 9951 and 8842, plus about 16,500 tons of coal. The introduction of the lighter aluminium hoppers has resulted in a heavier payload per wagon compared with the old steel wagons.

Dense fog near Gillette, Wyoming enhances this early morning photograph of passing BNSF coal trains travelling to and from the Powder River Basin coal mines. These mines supply power station coal to installations, too numerous to detail, in Texas, Michigan, Colorado, Illinois, Arkansas, Nebraska, Louisiana and Pennsylvania, as well as Ontario, Manitoba and British Columbia in Canada. Every day the UP operates up to 34 Powder River coal trains and the BNSF up to 20 trains. Providing the illumination and reflection is BNSF SD70MAC 9849.

The size of the Powder River Basin coal mine infrastructure has to be seen to be believed. The 13 major installations all have their own railroad access, mine buildings, machinery and storage silos. This view illustrates Eagle Butte mine, about 8 miles north east of Gillette. It produces from the surface over 20 million tons of sub bituminous low sulphur coal every year. Just the silos seen here can store 48,000 tons of coal and the trackwork allows for five unit trains to be held on site. Under threatening skies this trio of BNSF SD70MACs, 9910/8840/9977, find a brief patch of sunshine as they leave the mine in May 1999. This is a standard coal train formation comprising three high adhesion locomotives and a 20,000 ton gross train of coal but even this payload could one day be uneconomic when the stripping ratio (the ratio of coal to the waste overburden rock) becomes too great. It is a fascinating area and a brief visit is recommended even though the attraction is the volume of trains and not train variety!

COLORADO and the ROCKIES

To do justice to the trains and the scenery in Colorado would require a book in its own right so a mere taster is the best we can do here. In a photograph which confirms by way of locomotive livery mix that it post-dates the UP takeover of SP in 1996, it seems that UP have taken a leaf out of SP's book by producing a lash-up of extremely dirty locomotives. Even a flash of the late afternoon sunshine does not make this quintet of 4,400hp AC machines looked cared for. However the horsepower has not been skimped as the thunderous power rolls into Rollinsville with a massive westbound mixed manifest, while menacing mountains look on. The train is on the Moffat route, a few miles east of the 6.2 mile Moffat Tunnel under the Continental Divide, which is at an elevation of 9,239ft. The tunnel was built in 1928 saving 20 route miles and 2,000ft in altitude over the original route. Between Denver and Rollinsville there are no fewer than 30 tunnels, mountain railroading indeed and a clue to the state of the locomotives!

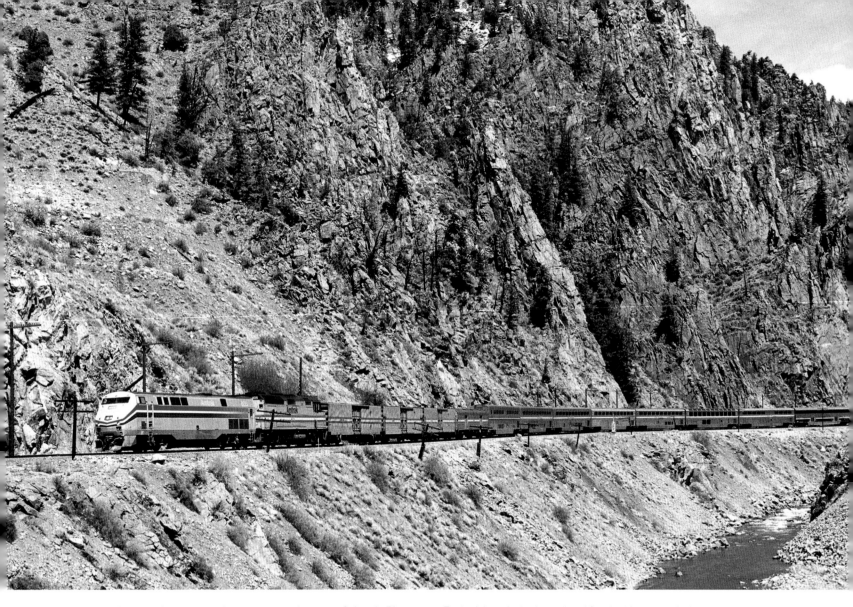

Located at 7,690ft, Byers Canyon is an 8 mile gorge on the upper Colorado River about 90 miles west of Denver. Highway 40 from Hot Sulphur Springs to Kremmling runs through the gorge, sharing the space with the river and the original Denver & Rio Grande Western Railroad. Running over an hour late the westbound 'California Zephyr' threads the jagged and formidable canyon in April 1995 behind P40DC 805 (now stored) and F40PHR 405. The view from the top deck of the following coaches must have been special indeed. Of the leading vehicles three will contain US Postal Services mail and parcels. (also see Page 12.)

To gain altitude out of the 'mile high city' of Denver trains climb from the Great Plains through what are colloquially know as the ten degree 'Big Ten' curves. Beyond Coal Creek there is a formidable ascent of the Rocky Mountains. In this May 1999 scene the famous westbound 'California Zephyr' is passing Blue Mountain Drive at the end of Coal Creek Canyon and will shortly be passing through the first of numerous tunnels. Heading the train are GE 'Genesis' P40 units 15 and 66 while a F40PH provides welcome support for the forthcoming climb. Amtrak was formed in 1971 under the 'Rail Passenger Service Act' when a nationwide rail system was created and dedicated to the provision of passenger services. The F40s were withdrawn between 2005 and 2010 and either sold for further service, scrapped, converted to baggage cab control cars ('cabbages') or stored.

A pair of interesting interlopers have popped-up between this pair of BN locomotives on 1 May 1995. Rolling into Aguilar, north of Trinidad, on the north to south 'Joint' line east of the Rockies, is a southbound merchandise train headed by BN SD40-2 8015, Ferrocarriles Nacionales de Mexico (FNM) U30C 8902, Montana Rail Link SD45-2XR 356 and GP50L 3111. The DRGW 'Joint' line from Denver to Pueblo was once narrow gauge and dates back to 1872. The ATSF reached Pueblo from Atchison, Kansas four years later in 1876. Gauge conversion followed in later years. Between 1914 and 1996 the railways of Mexico were owned by the government under the single name of FNM (see aside) but after a change to the constitution in 1996 the railways were gradually privatised and by 1999 the government had sold seven separate systems to private enterprise.

The contrast between the dry dusty foreground and the snow covered Rocky Mountains in the background is dramatic, as a coal train from the Antelope Mine in the Powder River Basin, Wyoming to Harrington Power Station, near Amarillo, Texas heads south a few miles north of Aguilar, Colorado. The uniform motive power consist comprises a trio of BNSF SD70MACs, 9542/9339/9417. What is so fascinating in the photograph are the two dark 'worms' in the top right background, which are distant northbound and southbound coal trains. Estimates vary widely but observers have reported as few as 4 trains per day traversing the line and a maximum of 30! The summit of the line is at Palmer Lake where an altitude of 7,200ft is reached.

During the recent past the now closed line over Tennessee Pass was the highest of the standard gauge transcontinental railway lines in the USA. The spectacular route over the Rocky Mountains reached the remarkable altitude of 10,239ft through the 2,550ft long Tennessee Pass Tunnel. During its final years the main payloads were coal and taconite. Although it is the end of April the temperature at Red Hill is bitterly cold as a seven locomotive consist powers a merchandise train through Eagle River Canyon. The SP/DRGW locomotives are Nos 5504/8506/8566/8364/6781/8353/7767, all but one being from the EMD stable and most being SD40-2 tunnel motors. The winter snows linger.

Below: In the Rocky Mountains and High Sierras black bears, brown bears and gizzly bears are not rare and they must be treated with great respect. Glacier National Park and the Canadian Rockies seem to be the locations where most confrontations take place. In the main the animals avoid humans but where food or cubs are concerned bears can attack and over the years there have been fatalities. This grizzly was taken from a public road in the Rocky Mountains while on a railway expedition.

With gradients as steep as 3 per cent just about every train working from Minturn to Pueblo (and vice versa) via the Tennessee Pass required huge amounts of motive power. Although these coal hoppers are empty a massive 9 locomotive lash-up was summoned for the journey over the Rocky Mountains. Approaching Red Hill are DRGW/SP locomotives 5503/5508/5505/5517/8629/8154/8161/5383/8701, on 29 April 1995. It was great to see a trio of Rio Grande liveried locomotives on the point nearly 8 years after the Anschutz Corporation, the owners of DRGW, purchased SP in 1988. The snow is a reminder of the altitude.

The bleak surroundings at Minturn are brought to life by another large Tennessee Pass block train of coal empties. In April 1995 eight SP EMD second generation locomotives comprising 8634/8566/8506/5504/8364/6875/9257/9384 throb their way out of town for either a Colorado or Utah coalfield and another load of coal for a hungry power station. There was a yard and a locomotive facility at Minturn as well as offices, a crew signing on point and a turning facility. However bad news was on its way for the line in 1997. In 1996 the UP took over the SP gifting the UP unlimited access to the SP/DRGW Moffat route, which although limited in capacity was much easier to work. Also the UP diverted much traffic over their main transcontinental route across Wyoming. Consequently traffic over Tennessee Pass dwindled to virtually nothing and the line closed. It has since been mothballed and there are no immediate signs of resuscitation. Subsequent landslides and washouts would now make this an expensive proposition.

COPPER COUNTRY

The rich mineral resources of Arizona include large areas of copper deposits. To move the mined ore railways provided an obvious solution. The longest line is the 54 mile Copper Basin Railway from Magma (about 40 miles south east of Phoenix) to Winkleman, plus a 7 mile branch from Ray Junction to Ray Mine. At the intermediate point of Hayden a junction was made with the San Manuel Arizona Railroad, which ran down to the smelter at San Manuel. From San Manuel a further Magma Arizona Copper Company line ran to Mammoth Copper Mine. The entire complex has been the subject of changes of ownership and the whims of the modern corporate world, including the filing of Chapter 11 bankruptcy by one company. Sadly as a result of all of this wrangling and international commodity prices the entire complex including the two railway lines from San Manuel closed on 25 June 1999. With Mammoth Mine in the far distance and prickly pear cacti in bloom Magma's ex-SP GP9 No 4 in its CSX style livery crosses Smelter Wash, on its way to San Manuel.

One of the great pieces of western USA railway infrastructure that has all but disappeared is the phenomena of the large wooden trestle. Possibly the best collection of structures in recent years could be found on Oregon branch lines, especially those serving the lumber industry, but many of these have now closed. Other outstanding examples were to be found at Mammoth, Arizona on the San Manuel Arizona Railroad Company (a subsidiary of Magma Copper Corporation), seen here. A long wait was necessary on 9 May 1995 to capture this view of four

GP38s 16/19/18/17 making their way across Mammoth Wash from San Manuel to Hayden, the timbers groaning under their 500 US ton combined weight. In 2007 the Environmental Protection Agency found "abnormally high pollutants in soil and air samples" (particularly arsenic, lead and copper) near Hayden, with obvious implications for mining operations. This line also closed in 1999, relegating such scenes to railway history.

It is 07.35 and the Magma Arizona Railway is already hard at work. Built by the Magma Copper Company as a narrow gauge line in 1915 it was converted to standard gauge in 1923. For decades the 30.2 mile line from the works at Superior, Arizona was used to haul cattle and copper to a junction made with the SP at Magma. In its later years loads of Perlite were hauled down the line in hopper wagons. In 1996, the year after this photograph was taken, the Australian mining giant Broken Hill Proprietary purchased the company and the line for $A3.2m and immediately suspended operations for a year. The line never reopened. The company was later resold to Resolution Copper, a subsidiary of London based Rio Tinto. In this delightful early morning cameo 1951-built ALCo RS3 No 9, originally Reading 520, passes the corrugated iron office building at Superior with four wagons of Perlite, ACFX 490373/324/351/418. One wonders what the security guard is now doing for a living.

A GLIMPSE of NEW MEXICO

Abo Canyon in New Mexico is situated at 5,410ft mainly in Socarro and Valencia Counties between the Los Pinos and Manzano Mountains. The BNSF main line runs through the canyon enabling eastbound trains to climb from Belen in the Rio Grande Valley to the higher plateau at Mountainair and Vaughn (no family connection!) and vice versa. Since its construction over a century ago the line through the canyon from Sais to Scholle has always been single and with increasing traffic in recent years this has caused bottlenecks. Accordingly in 2005 BNSF announced a massive $50m investment in doubling 4.5 miles of track through the canyon area. The work entails much grading and the construction of seven new viaducts. Rolling out of the canyon in April 2002 is this westbound 'earthworm' grain train powered by BNSF Dash 9-44CWs 5370 and 5439. The foreground 'mini-cliffs' have been created by erosion, caused by an adjacent wash.

Very few tourists to the area see this magnificent view of desert railroading, especially since enhanced security was introduced at the start of the upgrade works and following the detestable '9/11' attack. Against a typical New Mexico backdrop a stack/'pig' consist climbs into Abo Canyon and crosses Bridge #1 behind a wonderful lash-up of four motor diesels in pre-merger Santa Fe liveries comprising GP60 4014, B40-8W 554, GP60M 113, cabless GP60B 329 and GP60 4012. In the summer months these fluffy clouds combine to produce fierce thunderstorms, which produce the heaviest rainfall of the year. This vista now resembles a building site.

Right: A typical Abo Canyon scene from May 1995 finds a quartet of six motor Warbonnets powering a Chicago to Los Angeles TOFC hot-shot westward over Bridge #2 and towards Belen on the BNSF's southern transcontinental route. The four degree curves and a 1.25 per cent down grade in the canyon will limit the train to 40mph. This GE superpower is a cocktail of C44-9W and C40-8W locomotives, 642/821/931/899, able to tackle almost anything that nature cares to put in its way. At the time of writing the upgrade construction was continuing but at a slower pace due to the 2008-2010 recession. The double track should be ready for service by the end of 2011.

This lovely old SD9E 'Cadillac' was still at work in New Mexico on 1 May 1995 but at the head of an engineer's train rather than toiling at the head of a freight train over Donner Pass or trundling along the lumber branch lines of Oregon. Having been retired from SP service 4379 and 4438 were being leased by Great Western Leasing (GWRX) when photographed at the unlikely location of Raton depot. Work stained 4379 looked every bit of its 40 year age but despite its deplorable external condition evidence of its former maintenance location of Roseville could still be seen.

Raton Pass was on the old Santa Fe trail and was known as the 'gateway to the south west'. It was the only pass between the southern end of the Rocky Mountains and the Sangre de Cristo Mountains. Located in New Mexico Territory (which did not become a State until 1912) the pass attained an elevation of 7,834ft, which presented a challenge to the railway builders. Nevertheless the ATSF won a battle with the DRGW entering New Mexico in 1878, with the objective of linking the plains of Kansas to the Gulf of Mexico where the port of Guyamas, Mexico would give access to the Orient. After the opening of the Belen Cut-off in 1907 traffic over Raton reduced and now, over 100 years later, it is absolutely minimal with BNSF reputedly not using the line, which is now owned by the State of New Mexico. However for the moment Amtrak's 'Southwest Chief' still uses the route. In a scene unlikely to ever be repeated a massive merchandise train slogs up the climb to Raton from Trinidad behind ATSF SD40-2 5029, SD45-2 5830, SDP40F cowl rebuild 5254 and SD40-2 5050. The snow covered Rockies are in the distant background.

67

RAIL TRAVELLERS

While understandably the majority of this tome illustrates freight trains there are still a number of surviving passenger train services in parts of the wild west. Here we show just a glimpse of the immense variety of workings. The Californian Pacific Coast line north of San Diego and both east and west from Santa Barbara is spectacular and affords passengers great views of the ocean and the occasional oil rig. On the delightful late afternoon of 6 May 2005 Amtrak's backlit southbound ten coach 'Coast Starlight' is nearing the end of its long journey from Seattle, Washington to Los Angeles as it hugs the coastal strip near Carpinteria behind Amtrack GE P42DC 115 and a GE P32B. Railway photographers should note that there is 'no parking any time' on the adjacent Highway 101!

Right: Amtrak's 'Pacific Surfliner' runs between San Diego and San Luis Obispo via Santa Barbara. The service has recently increased with 12 round trips per weekday out of San Diego. At peak times the service is used by commuters bound for greater Los Angeles. The mist has retracted from the notoriously foggy coastline, at least in the mornings, and here shrouds the coastal range of mountains at Santa Barbara. Pausing at the station is F59PHI 457 with a northbound working comprising bi-level Bombardier coaches.

In England 'Health & Safety at Work' legislation would almost certainly condemn this dangerous looking practise whereby an older pensioner couple are using a primitive wooden stool in order to reach *terra firma* from their comfortable Amtrak coach. The platform at Colfax, California does not extend to this doorway as a male passenger is about to take a tentative step from the eastbound 'California Zephyr' in May 2007, while the female conductor assists his wife with the luggage.

Metrolink was formed in 1991 and since then the network has greatly expanded to include 388 route miles and 55 stations. Routes are centred on Los Angeles running on lines to San Bernardino, Riverside, Oceanside and Lancaster. In 2009 the weekday ridership increased to 38,400. The Santa Clarita Line is now called the 'Antelope Valley Line' with services now operated by Amtrak staff, the previous provider being Veolia Transport. The services utilise 23 EMD F59PH locomotives and Bombardier bi-level coaches. In April 2000 868 has an off-peak load of only two coaches as it calls at Santa Clarita. The livery is 'white with periwinkle blue stripes'!

Right: Amtrak's 'San Joaquin' runs from Oakland or Sacramento to Bakersfield via Stockton and Fresno. The lengthy journey down the Central Valley takes between 6hrs 5mins and 6hrs 15mins, depending on whether a particular train starts or completes its journey at Oakland or Sacramento. There are half a dozen trains in each direction daily, two of which serve Sacramento. All trains have various bus connections between stations and places of note and centres of population. In October 1995 F59PHI 2005 accelerates its southbound train away from Stockton past milepost 1118.

The old 49.5 mile San Francisco & San Jose Railroad dates back to 1864. The line opened to cope with the growing transport requirements of the burgeoning South Bay area. From 1870 until 1982 passenger services were run by Southern Pacific connecting all major towns down the west side of the bay, including San Bruno, San Mateo, Redwood City and Palo Alto but in 1982 services were transferred to Caltrans. From 1985 Geeps hired from SP were replaced by 20 new F40PH-2 locomotives with the stock also being replaced by new stainless steel coaches. The new 'Caltrains' were a success but in 1992 services were administered by an independent agency called the Joint Powers Board. Photographed at San Jose Cahill Street station, now Diridon, in 1987 are F40PF-2s 905 and 917, which have both arrived from San Francisco. Down the road at Lenzen Avenue is a roundhouse and engine depot.

Left: These aesthetically displeasing coaches with apparently tiny windows were in everyday operation between Oakland/Sacramento and Bakersfield in the summer of 1994. Hustling the northbound train along arrow straight track through Escalon in the vegetable and fruit growing Central Valley is Amtrak F40PH 309, now scrapped. Amtrak acquired 215 of these locomotives between 1976 and 1988. Escalon is a town with a population of just over 7,000 and it is located in San Joaquin County between Modesto and Stockton.

B.C. PACIFIC COAST

Following Captain Vancouver's explorations in 1792 a settlement was created at Burrard Inlet in the early 19th century. The town of Vancouver was once known as Gastown and later Granville before adopting its current name in 1886, after its effective founder. The city has traditionally had considerable links with Great Britain, rivalled only by Victoria on Vancouver Island. However due to heavy dilution by immigration over recent decades 35 per cent of the population is now foreign born, mainly in China and southern Asia. The city boasts Canada's largest and most diversified port and also the second largest 'China Town' in North America. This photographs shows some of the dock sidings on a quiet Sunday morning in October 1991. Later in the day rebuilt CP Rail switcher SW1200RS 1206 may be required to earn its keep.

Dramatic lighting at Mission at 18.40 on 18 September 1997 as the 'West Coast Express' from Vancouver rolls into town behind locomotive 902. The WCE is a premium commuter service that has been in operation since 1995. The growing system presently comprises 43 route miles and ridership is on the increase. On the main line from Mission five push/pull trains per day operate in each direction, the five morning trains to Vancouver making their return journey at evening commuter times. During off peak periods passenger journeys are supplemented by bus services, all run by the TransLink operators. The trains comprise between 4 and 9 Bombardier bi-level cars hauled by F59PHI locomotives. The locomotives are maintained by VIA Rail and the track by CP Rail.

Man made structures dominate the scene at New Westminster, beside the Fraser River, another British Columbia city carrying a name with historical British connotations. At the top of the picture an ex-Vancouver Skytrain working to Surrey is seen against a dramatic sky as it competes with road and rail traffic while crossing the impressive Skytrain Bridge. Behind is the 1937 built Pattullo Bridge for road traffic, while the less significant railway bridge can be seen below the other two. In the foreground are three wide cab Canadian National Railways (CN) GP40-2Ws built between 1974 and 1976, headed by 9443.

Right: In total the Port of Vancouver trades with 130 countries and has a turnover of C$75bn. The main ferry terminal for Vancouver Island is at Tsawwassen on the Delta, which was purpose-built in 1959. Most people want to travel to Victoria from the City of Vancouver but the terminal is 17 miles to the south, which is curious logic. One of Vancouver's major freight terminals is Roberts Bank Superport. Included in the complex are Deltaport Container terminal and Westshore Terminal, which is the busiest coal export facility in the whole of North America, exporting 21 million tons per annum. The coal comes largely from Alberta and Wyoming and on the horizon a pair of CP Rail SD40-2s are easing a massive load towards Westshore, as seen from the first deck of the Vancouver Island ferry.

Left: The over four hour wait to photograph this BN freight train passing White Rock on Semiahmoo Bay was so long that the tide went out in the process! The southbound train is only 3.4 miles from the Canadian/United States border and it is running along an old Great Northern route that is now in the hands of the BNSF. The just visible station opened in 1913 but services were discontinued in 1971. Heading a typical load of lumber and other merchandise towards the US are BN liveried GP38-2 2309, GP39 2763 and GP40 3520, on 19 September 1997.

Right: This International tractor driver knows that he is in for a long wait judging by the position of his Wellington boot! An outbound coal train from Roberts Bank, about 15 miles south of Vancouver, slowly passes an inbound train of double stacks destined for nearby Deltaport. The switching power is being provided by a veteran Omnitrax SD9E 1750 (ex-SP 4375). CP Rail, CN and BNSF all have access to the terminals.

76

Prior to 1972 the rail route heading north from Vancouver was operated by the old Pacific Great Eastern Railway. The 466 mile railway line from North Vancouver to Prince George started life in 1912. From 1972 until 1984 the operators were British Columbia Railways and from 1984 until 2004 it was BC Rail. The track and other assets are now publicly owned and CN acquired a 999 year operating lease for the princely sum of C$1 in 2004! Between 1974 and 2001 the route between

North Vancouver and Squamish was used by the 'Royal Hudson' steam train excursions. In May 2001, in the BC Rail era, C40-8M 4609 heads two sister locomotives through some dense foliage between Squamish and Horseshoe Bay with a southbound freight. The main commodity on the line is timber and wood pulp from lumber mills. Of interest is the Canadian practise of placing the warning bell above the windscreen.

SHORT LINES

The so called short lines in the wild west can produce some of the most fascinating operations imaginable, often traversing difficult terrain with normally smaller and older motive power that has long been pensioned off by the Class 1 railroads. Photographing them is always a challenge due to the absence of a specific timetable compounded in some cases by the infrequency of trains. The little gem depicted here is the Quincy Railroad Company that comprises a 3.27 mile branch from the Quincy Lumber Company at Bell Lane, Quincy, California to Quincy Junction on the former WP, now UP, main line. The line is an old one, dating back to July 1909. Associated with Sierra Pacific Industries, activities have recently been impacted by the national forest policy, environmental issues and a shifting economy resulting in the closure of one local plant. In October 1995 the power was provided by 1942 ALCo S1 No 4 but this locomotive has since been retired to the railroad museum at nearby Portola. The line had been carrying 1,000 freight cars per annum and here three of them are being switched beside some prepared timber.

Another old line that until comparatively recent times employed ALCo switchers was the Stockton Terminal & Eastern Railroad. The railway operates 25 miles of track in the Stockton, California area, connecting with the UP, BNSF and Central California Traction Company. Some trackage runs through the residential streets of the city. Its longest route to Linden has been mothballed for several years and is presently non operational. Seen here at the ST&E's Stockton depot are S1 505 of 1942, S2 560 of 1950 and S2 557 of 1943. Operations are now in the hands of a SW1200 switcher and ALCo 506 has found a permanent home at the WP Railroad Museum at Portola.

Below: One of the hottest locations ever visited, in temperature terms and especially in the summer months, is Parker, Arizona home of the Arizona & California Railway, which is owned by the Park Sierra Rail Group. The former ATSF 1907-1910 built line is hardly 'short' running from Cadiz, California via Parker to Wickenburg, Arizona, with a long branch to Ripley, a total of 297 route miles. Having not been used since 2007 the Ripley branch has recently been closed. The A&CR began operations in 1991 employing locomotives decanted from Class 1 companies. The locomotives are normally immaculate and heading this line-up at Parker is 1963 built GP30 3002, which is ex-OHCR, CSXT 4217 and C&O 3023. In the summer temperatures reach an *average* of 111F (44C) during the day and a modest 84F (29C) at night!

Right: One of the finest little railroads in the west was the Amador Central Railroad Company that ran through the attractive Californian foothills of the Sierra Nevada range from Ione, where a connection was made with the SP, to a lumber company and railroad depot at Martell, a distance of 11.79 miles. The line started life as the Ione & Eastern in 1904 becoming the ACR in 1909. Passenger services were operated until the early 1930s. Lumber operations have continually changed hands including 1946 Winton Lumber Company, 1964 American Forest Products, 1988 Georgia Pacific and 1997 Sierra Pacific Industries. For many years the line was operated by 1951/52 built Baldwins 9 and 10 but they were replaced in 1995 by this SW1200, No 11. Operations ceased in 1997 but the line reopened in 1999 and was renamed the Amador Foothills Railroad. The railway continued to haul lumber products down the hill until 2004 when the line and the mill closed. The track was then used by privately owned speeders but that too came to an end in March 2010. In this attractive view No 11 curves its way to Martell at Sutter Creek Ranchos Road in October 1995 with four empty box cars.

This would seem to be great work, if you can get it! A member of staff of the Modesto and Empire Traction Company enjoys the Californian sunshine aboard locomotives 600/601 as he takes in the view between Empire Junction, where there is an interchange with BNSF, and the Beard Industrial Estate. The Class 3 short line had interurban origins and dates back to 1911 but such operations ceased in 1918. Steam traction was finally ousted by diesel in 1953. The MET now operates 5 miles of 'main' branch line and 28 miles of industrial sidings. Since 1947 the company has operated up to nine GE 70 ton switchers, normally in double headed mode, as seen here in October 1995. The company now runs eco-friendly 'GenSets' but upon retirement, having served the company for an impressive 62 years (1947 to 2009), No 600 was preserved by the company for sentimental reasons. The Beard family have owned the line since the early days through their Land & Investment Company.

Left: An original railway depot dating back to 1909, a colourful 'Geep' locomotive (GP16 93 – ex-Seaboard 1850) from the 1960s and a 'photographer's' sky make an irresistible combination at Sante Fe, New Mexico in May 1995. Despite Santa Fe being incorporated within the legendary ATSF name the town was not directly served by that company's main line, instead being accessed by a branch line from Lamy. Since 1992 the Santa Fe Southern has performed a dual role of running tourist and dining trains along the route while also conveying BNSF freight cars for Sante Fe customers. Lamy is named after Jean-Baptiste Lamy, a Catholic priest who became Archbishop for the Territory.

The Apache Railway is a Class 2 short line that has become well known in railfan circles for running a fleet of ALCo locomotives, which are kept in immaculate condition. The 38 mile freight line runs from Snowflake, Arizona via Snowflake Paper Mill to Holbrook where it connects with the BNSF transcontinental main line. The railway was incorporated in 1917 and it operated passenger as well as freight services until the 1950s. The line once extended beyond Snowflake to McNary but that section closed in 1984. Over the years there have been changes of ownership and in April 2008 the line and the Snowflake paper recycling mill, then owned by Abitibi Consolidated, was purchased by the Catalyst Paper Corporation, a Canadian company. Climbing hard towards Snowflake Junction with a trailing load of 6,500 tons are 81/84/800/82/83, four ALCo C420s and a single RS36, all of 1960s manufacture.

Right: It was up at the crack of dawn in October 1995 to photograph the California Northern Railroad at Tracy, California. With the golden sun shining on former CNW 4412, a leased GP15-1 running as CFNR 101 (and now on the UP roster as UPY543), a West Side Line trainload for Los Banos is being assembled. The company commenced operations in 1993 and now runs half a dozen short lines at Suisun and Schellville 24 miles, Napa 7.1 miles, Vallejo 5.9 miles, West Valley 110.7 miles, Hamilton 11.4 miles and West Side 57.2 miles. The entire CFNR operation was purchased by Rail America in 2002, a company that runs 40 railroads in 27 States. The company now operates the latest eco-friendly GenSet N-ViroMotives.

Throughout the great American and Canadian west there are a considerable number of preserved lines and tourist railways. Largely manned by volunteers these railroads perform herculean tasks not only in giving pleasure to thousands but in preserving vintage machinery, often in working condition. Such lines are not the subject of this volume but this photograph has been included as a dedication to all such railroads. The Sierra Railway and the Railtown 1897 State Historic Park operation at Jamestown have been famous for decades in that Hollywood has used the line to great effect on numerous occasions. Movies ranging from the classic 1952 'High Noon' with Gary Cooper, Grace Kelly, Lloyd Bridges and Lee Van Cleaf to 'Back to the Future 3' in 1990 with Michael J Fox were part made on the Sierra Railroad, not to mention such TV series as 'Little House on the Prairie'. Acquired from the Concorde Naval Weapons Station in 1991 beautifully presented ALCo MRS-1 (RSX4) 613 is seen returning from Sierra Rock siding to Jamestown in 1995.

The Sierra's freight operation once ran from Oakdale to Tuolumne, a distance of 57.4 miles, and in years gone by there were other branches, including a line from Jamestown to Angels Camp. However the branches closed and in later years the 'main' line was cut back to a lumber mill at Standard. In 2008 the Sierra bought the BNSF branch from Oakdale to Riverbank, where it connects to the Class 1 road. Since 1999 dining trains have run on the Sierra RR out of Oakdale by the Sierra Entertainment Group. For many years the standard freight train motive power was supplied by a trio of 1950s built Baldwin S12s. In June 1994 a very rare view was captured; Oakdale based Baldwin 42 being turned on the original 1897 Jamestown roundhouse turntable, to equalise locomotive tire (tyre) wear. The Baldwins have now been pensioned off in favour of a GP9 but at least the freight still runs, serving intermediate points such as the Sierra Pacific lumber mill at Chinese Camp.

NORTHERN CALIFORNIA

In this blast from the past a vintage consist arrives at the Permante installation in the hills west of San Jose, California. When photographed on 29 June 1987 the 16.2 mile Vasona branch enjoyed a daily freight that ran early evening. Heading the train around the final curve is rebuilt SP SD9E 4392 and SW1500 2671 with a couple of other EMD 'espee' locomotives in support. Within a year Southern Pacific Transportation would be purchased by Rio Grande Industries (which owned the Denver & Rio Grande Western Railroad) for $1.2bn, with Philip Anschutz directing the transaction. The main question then being asked by railfans was "would SP locomotives become any cleaner"?

One of the author's favourite SP branch lines is from Galt to Ione, California. At Ione the SP connected with the Amador Central Railroad. The SP north to south main line through Galt dates back to 1869/70 but the Ione branch was built considerably later. The branch crossed the Central California Traction's Stockton to Sacramento line at Herald via a 90 degree crossover. In years gone by the line served Rancho Seco nuclear power station and a china clay works at Indian Hill but in recent years the main traffic was lumber (until the ACR closed, see Page 79), bulk clay and crushed rock. In 1994 trains ran thrice weekly. The gentle whine of a brace of SP GP9s, 3336 and 3382, fills the still summer air as they run through golden grass on the approach to Carbondale Road with just five eastbound cars in tow.

With such a focus on the classic Californian rail routes of Tehachapi, Cajon, Donner and the Feather River other lines tend to get overlooked photographically, even though they have a great deal to offer. With the Vaca Mountains looming in the background a wonderfully mixed and colourful 53 car freight from the Sacramento direction is headed by a pair of UP C40-8s, 9281 and 9163, as it approaches Morrow, near Bahia north of Benicia, making for Richmond on 8 October 1998. The famous Napa Valley Wine Train operates a few miles to the north west of this location.

At over a mile long and 135ft above the water line the Suisun Bay Bridge between Benicia and Martinez is a formidable structure. The bridge dates back to 1930 and before its construction the Central Pacific operated a train ferry across the mighty Sacramento River, increased in size at this point by the nearby confluence with the San Joaquin River. The bay and the bridge were named after the Suisunes, a nearby tribe of Native Americans. The area was famous for many years as a massive graveyard for retired and redundant US Navy vessels. A northbound mixed manifest with scrap metal wagons leading adheres to the speed limit as it crosses the muddy waters and makes for Roseville headed by UP SD50 5038, SD60M 6158 and SD40-2 3631.

This colourful BNSF formation is heading south on the main north to south 'I-5 Corridor' route south of Mount Shasta but north of Redding in May 2001. Electro-Motive SD60 9044 leads Santa Fe Warbonnet SD75M 8244 and renumbered Bluebonnet 6729 (ex-5070). As usual in this part of the west a significant part of the train comprises various timber products from the Pacific Northwest, including

British Columbia. The Warbonnet paint scheme originated in 1937 when it was first applied to Santa Fe 'E' units. It was reintroduced by Mike Haverty, the then new President of ATSF, in 1989. It was immensely attractive but weathered badly unless well maintained.

The Shasta Lakes area is something special in both scenic and recreational terms, a fact that is recognised by thousands of campers and boating fans during the season. Part of the lakes complex is artificial in that they were formed by the construction of Shasta Dam. The scale of the lakes should not be underestimated. They cover an area of 30,000 acres, have a shore line 365 miles long and in a good wet year can reach a depth of over 500ft. The original railway route through the area was built before the creation of the lakes, at a much lower level than the present line. One of the impressive structures of the 'new' alignment is Salt Creek Trestle, the creek eventually providing an additional flow to the Sacramento River. Heading south and about to enter Tunnel #8 in May 2007 is a mixed manifest with some chunky UP power up front in the shape of C44AC 5634 and three SD70Ms, 5171/4585/4502. In recent years water levels have dropped revealing the infrastructure of the original railway, especially around old Tunnel #6.

The most famous location on the rail route through California's Diablo Mountain range is Altamont Pass. The line was part of the original 1869 Sacramento to San Francisco Bay extension of the first transcontinental rail route. Sadly the old CP/SP line was abandoned in 1984 (visible on the hillside below the trestle). The remaining track is part of the Western Pacific Feather River Route, now UP territory. Even though it is only June the green grasses are already turning to gold in the absence of any measurable precipitation and increasing temperatures. Oakland bound American President Line double stacks have passed the summit and are now in descent towards Livermore. Providing the dynamics on this day are UP C41-8W 9539 and SD60M 6282. Visible on the distant hilltop beneath the trestle are a row of power generating windmills, just part of a 7,000 population in the area.

BIG SKY COUNTRY

The BNSF route over Marias Pass in the north of the State of Montana climbs to 5,213ft in an area to the south of Glacier National Park. The railway runs between the Lewis and Clark National Forest and the Flathead National Forest. The alignment of the railway line was proposed by John Frank Stevens the principal engineer of the Great Northern Railroad in 1889. It is now part of BNSF's northern transcontinental route. Part of the route is bordered with dense conifers such as that seen near Belton at an altitude of 3,169ft. In May 2001 BNSF Dash 9-44CW 4932 heads east from Pasco, Washington and is seen climbing through the forest with a modicum of EMD support.

Left: One of the main rail routes running across the State of Montana was operated by the Northern Pacific Railroad. It was absorbed into Burlington Northern in the early 1970s but in 1987 the line from Huntley, Montana to Sandpoint in Idaho and branches, amounting in all to over 900 route miles, was acquired by Montana Rail Link under the direction of Dennis Washington. MRL is a Class 2 railroad and the largest privately owned line in the USA. The company employs some 900 staff and they have a roster of over 100 locomotives. One of the toughest climbs on the largely single track main line is over Bozeman Pass, especially with a head wind and in pouring rain. With the photographer in 'never give up' mode BNSF Dash 9-44CW 4944 and SD40-2 8037 grind up the climb at East Muir with a maximum load for the power available, in May 1999.

The main MRL function is to provide crews and helper locomotives for through BNSF freights from Jones Junction, east of Billings, to Sandpoint, Idaho. However there is plenty of local traffic and MRL has trackage rights through to Spokane, Washington. MRL connects with BNSF at Spokane, and Laurel and Garrison in Montana as well as UP at Sandpoint, Idaho. The railroad is shifting about 45 million tons of merchandise per annum and it owns nearly 2,000 freight cars. Against the blue hills of Helena National Forest the Livingston to Helena local comprising just five wagons heads west behind a pair of ex-DRGW/SP 'Geeps', with GP35 404 leading.

The City of Helena is the Capital of Montana and is located at an elevation of 4,058ft. The average daytime temperature in January is 29F but in July it rises to a respectable 85F. The town grew rapidly after gold was discovered in the area in 1864, the territory becoming a State in 1889. The population is about 30,000 but in terms of the total catchment area it is nearer 75,000. William Cornish the MRL Roadmaster is a personal friend of the writer and he lives in nearby Clancy.

Against a staggering backdrop where mountains such as Elkhorn Peak run to over 9,000ft, way above the cloud base on this day, a heavy mixed manifest climbs the 2.2 per cent grade out of Helena at West Tobin in May 1999. An impressive seven locomotive combination provides the head end power, with MRL liveried F45XR 390 on the point of a Santa Fe/BN liveried cocktail.

The MRL main line over Mullan Pass is as rugged as it gets. One has to admire the efforts of Lieutenant John Mullan an Army engineer who crossed the pass in March 1854 leading to the construction of a primitive road in 1860. At the top of the pass is Mullan Tunnel, where the line crosses the Rocky Mountains on the Continental Divide at 5,566ft. The tunnel is over 3,000ft long but throughout its life it has been susceptible to rock falls and partial roof collapses. Major remedial work was carried out in July 2009. In fabulous surroundings this westbound is seen crossing Austin Creek Trestle and filling the mountains with sound, as half a dozen six motor second generation MRL locomotives provide the grunt. The dirt road on the left marks the course of the original 'over the top' rail route.

Right: For nearly 20 years MRL relied solely upon secondhand EMD locomotives from various Class 1 roads, including a large number of the often spurned 20 cylinder SD45s. However in 2005 the company acquired the first of 16 new build SD70AC locomotives. The fleet is maintained in shops at Livingston, Montana and the mainly single track (with passing sidings) CTC main line is controlled from Missoula. The MRL training car and a pair of dome coaches have been incorporated in this smart looking eastbound freight, seen crossing Austin Creek Trestle behind ex-ATSF SD45-2 309, ex-BN (formerly ex-GN) SD45XR 351 and ex-BN GP9 113. Note the traces of snow on the hills.

PRICE RIVER CANYON

Right: Utah's Price River Canyon route has its origins in the DRGW, which arrived in Helper with a narrow gauge railway in 1881/2 as part of the company's ambitions to link Denver with Provo and Salt Lake City. Helper was named as the location where 'helper' locomotives were added to trains for the climb over the Wasatch Mountains. Standard gauge conversion followed in 1893. The highlight of the route is the formidable 7,477ft Soldier Summit, which features a 2 per cent grade to the east and the west with a 2.4 per cent gradient in places. Thistle, Utah is located about 65 miles south east of Salt Lake City. It was the site of a massive landslip in 1983, which completely blocked Thistle Creek, Soldier Creek and the Spanish Fork River, and demolished the railway and highway. The railway closed for 3 months and the highway for 7 months, resulting in a new alignment for the old DRGW. Approaching the site of the most costly landslide in US history is a massive downhill coal drag, with SP AC4400CWs 378/168/222 providing the necessary brake force.

An evil sky greets the photographer at East Helena, while recording a pair of WATCO switchers, including SW1200 WATX 207 (originally NP148). WATCO Transport Services operate 21 short lines throughout the USA and they also have 21 contracted industrial switching locations. In this case it is the business premises of the American Chemet Group, which was incorporated in 1946. Amongst other substances they produce cuprous zinc and cupric oxide at their Smelter Road, East Helena plant and they have the marketing legend of 'Made in Montana – Sold to the World'. Works sidings are connected to the MRL. WATX 207 later passed into the hands of Webb Asset Management (WAMX).

The curvature of the line in the heart of the Price River Canyon, seen here, is rivalled by the Gilluly Loops on the western side of Soldier Summit. The summit is the fifth highest on a US main line, behind Tennessee Pass (now closed), Moffat Tunnel, Sherman Hill and Raton Pass. The Price River originates on the Wasatch Plateau in central Utah and the railway follows its course for some distance, which is precisely what this Utah Railway coal train is doing as it makes its way west at Kyune. From 1991 the Utah railway power has been supplied by Morrison Knudsen and on 24 April 1995 leasers 9008/cowl F45 5527/9004/9002 will be in 'run 8' power mode at this point of their journey. The three Utah Railway liveried engines are all rebuilt SD40-2Ms and started life with the C&O. The F45 is ex-ATSF.

There are few depot shots in this compilation but it impossible to exclude this view of the Utah Railway's installation, which is located in a breathtakingly beautiful setting at Martin, seen here. The scale and colour of the surrounding cliffs and mountains is truly awesome, making a lasting impression on the visitor. Here SD40-2Ms 9009/9007/9006/9004, all former CSXT locomotives, pose for photography between duties. As already mentioned from 1991 to 2001 the Utah Railway leased 9001 to 9011 from Morrison Knudsen, who operated the railroad for 10 years. The Utah Railway serves coal mines at Wildcat, Wattis, King Mohrland, Hiawatha and Panther. The railway owns only 45 miles of track but it has running rights from Grand Junction, Colorado to Provo, Utah a distance of 423 miles. The Class 3 company is now owned by Genesee & Wyoming Incorporated and it hauls 90,000 car loads of coal per annum.

Left: Utah coal trains operate all year round whatever the weather. In the depths of Winter the demand for coal increases as power consumption escalates. The entire Price River area is known for its coal mines, where the mineral was first discovered in 1875. In 1900 there was a terrible disaster at the nearby Winter Quarters Mine when 200 miners perished. This view shows the loader for Schofield Mine in Clear Creek Canyon, some 15 miles from the main line at Colton. Other mines on the branch line include Valcam and Skyline. Three SP AC4400CW locomotives, 341/317/182, have just arrived through the snow with empties from Provo. The train will soon be loading in slow speed control mode.

Below: This small reproduction has been included simply to show the juxtaposition of Provo locomotive depot to the impressive Wasatch Mountain range. With the 11,068ft Provo Peak as a backdrop UP SW10s 1228 and 1220 (both rebuilt EMD switchers) rest between duties in the depths of a Utah winter.

Right: The temperature has plummeted in the depths of Price River Canyon and just about everything other than the fast flowing river is frozen, including the photographer! This was always DRGW country and it was great to find Rio Grande liveried locomotives on the point. This solid tunnel motor lash-up including SD40T-2s 5379/5413/5380/5382 is making its way down to Castle Rock in the region of the Nolan Tunnels. The mixed manifest train will pause at Helper but will then continue on its way to Denver, Colorado. Such sights already belong to railway history even though recorded within the past 15 years. The last DRGW tunnel motor, 5371, which lasted in service until 2008, was donated by UP to the railway museum at Ogden in August 2009, a happy ending indeed.

CAJON

Right: With the possible exception of Tehachapi, the railroads of Cajon probably attract the majority of enthusiasts who enjoy train watching and photography in southern California. In 25.6 miles the railway climbs from 1,073ft to 3,823ft a mean gradient of 2 per cent, which in terms of the original 1885 Track 1 increases to 3 per cent in parts. The scenery at Cajon is not as attractive as Tehachapi but traffic levels are higher and to the west the San Gabriel Mountains overlook the scene. The sun sets early in the lower pass at Cajon as it dips behind the surrounding hills. With part of Mount Baldy as a backdrop this stack train will have the brakes firmly applied and the head end power will be in full dynamic braking mode as the ensemble crosses the San Andreas fault line on 2 April 1996. A quartet of dependable EMD locomotives led by ATSF 5167/5098/5166 and an unidentified example briefly head north east while travelling south west on the more northerly Track 2.

The Book Cliffs are a remarkable geological phenomena. Composed of sedimentary materials the cliffs extend for over 200 miles, the longest continuous escarpment in the world. The cliffs facilitate study of the great stages in the evolution of the world itself. Their altitude ranges from 4,500ft to 8,000ft and 70 per cent of the total area is under the control of the Bureau of Land Management. What is extremely unfortunate is that permits are granted for so called hunters to gun down unarmed elk and mule deer, who then have the temerity to call their repugnant activity sport! However that should not prevent enjoyment of landscapes such as this scene near Thompson, Utah. On 27 April 1995 an eastbound SP TOFC hot-shot, headed by three GP60 racehorses, 9659/9783/9601, speed past millions of years of erosion on their way to Colorado and beyond.

Left: On the right is the second track through Cajon, which was constructed in 1913 with a maximum grade of 2.2 per cent. At this point Tracks 1 and 2 are some distance apart. In 2008, 95 years later, a third line was built by BNSF to increase capacity on the hill, resulting in the single line on the right becoming double. However between those dates another addition to the railways of Cajon took place. In 1968 the SP completed construction of their 'Palmdale Cut-off' giving direct access from Tehachapi and Mojave to San Bernardino and their 'Sunset Route'. At the time it was heralded as the longest stretch of new railroad construction for over a quarter of a century. The grade from West Colton to the 3,854ft summit at Hiland is also 2.2 per cent. Rounding Sullivan's Curve, named after railway photographer Herb Sullivan, a pre-war exponent of the art, is a mixed manifest heading for West Colton yard behind SP SD70M 9801, SD45T-2 9314 and another locomotive. The curve is distinctive for its strange eroded rock formations.

Above: There was a terrible smash at 05.20 on 14 December 1994 when a westbound Santa Fe train headed by B40-8 576, FP45u 96, GP60M 144 and SDF45 5976 ran away from the summit. The train gathered speed and despite using cab communications it smashed into the back of a slow moving UP coal train just below Highway 138 between Alray and Cajon. At the rear of that train were UP SD40-2 helpers 3341 and 3354. Train crews jumped clear but all six locomotives and some wagons burned for many hours. There were rumours of sabotage, leading to the erection of high security fencing at summit. This is all that remained of ATSF GP60M 144.

Cajon Pass between the San Gabriel and San Bernardino Mountains was used by the Mormons back in 1851. It is therefore fitting that the rocks in the background of this shot were dubbed 'The Mormon Rocks'. Threading the rocks on 3 April 1996 this freight is heading south towards San Bernardino behind SP Cotton Belt GP60 9653 and a trio of six motor machines comprising 8631/7345/8337. It should be mentioned that in western railway circles the terms such as 'westbound' or 'eastbound' relate to overall journey direction rather than the specific direction of travel at a certain location. Such descriptions can become very confusing to the layman or visitor when they observe a westbound train heading east!

Near to the summit the two tracks traditionally used by ATSF and UP come together but since this photograph was taken on 1 March 1995 a third track has been added, on the right of this alignment. This new track comprises 42,000 concrete ties (sleepers), it is 16 miles long and construction involved daylighting Tunnels #1 and #2, subsequently requiring the removal over one million tons of earth. The project took four years to complete. Here Amtrak's eastbound 'Desert Wind' nears the end of its long climb behind GE P40 'Genesis' 831. This train no longer runs but the Los Angeles to Chicago 'Southwest Chief' still passes this way. The I-15 highway to Las Vegas runs through the hills top left.

The lower reaches of Cajon Pass can be affected by strong Santa Anna winds and on occasions a creeping fog drifts up from the Los Angeles basin. At higher elevations such as Frost, seen here, just south of Victorville, the sun shines more often. At this location there is a fascinating piece of trackwork where the eastbound and westbound tracks cross each other and on occasions it is possible to capture two trains in one frame. Here a westbound ATSF freight passes an eastbound UP example. The leading locomotives are in pristine condition, always a good advertisement for the company. Glowing C40-8 913 heads immaculate SF30C 9526 (a class of rebuilds that would become extinct on BNSF by 1998) plus BN cabless booster B30-7A 4057 and B40-8W 574.

GHOST TOWN

From the well trodden paths of southern California our journey now takes us to the remote ghost town of Modena, Utah – although the 28 inhabitants may object to that description! The old town is situated at 5,476ft, just 9.4 miles from the Nevada border, and is located on the UP Los Angeles to Salt Lake City rail route. Indeed the growth of the town in its early years was heavily influenced by the arrival of the railroad.

Modena is an unincorporated community within Iron County and it enjoys the luxury of a Post Office, which doubles as a general store and gas (petrol) station. Raising the dust as it hustles through town at 09.43 on 16 April 1997 with an eastbound 'K Line' double stacker are UP 6283 and 5989 (ex-CNW), wide and narrow cab versions of the SD60.

Modena is probably named after the well known town in Italy. The Utah version is located on the southern fringe of the Escalante Desert, about half way between Caliente, Nevada and Cedar City, Utah. The withdrawal of steam traction from the UP had a very negative impact on the town, especially in terms of employment. By 1990 there were only 80 residents and now just five families remain. Looking like the remains of a Hollywood 'Western' film set is the old and abandoned Lund Hotel and general store. Brigham J Lund and two partners set up business in town in 1899. A visit to Modena to soak-up the atmosphere is highly recommended. With the crossing bell clanging a pair of UP C40-8s highball it through town on the main line and head towards Great Salt Lake country.

IMAGES of IDAHO and BEYOND

Ask people what they know about the State of Idaho and many will answer "potatoes"! There is a grain of substance in such a reply because the State relies heavily on agriculture for its financial well being. The weather, soil and elevation in Idaho are ideal growing conditions for the 30 types of potato produced in the State, with the Russet Burbank being the best known variety. This International 1460 (with Axial Air Flow) combined harvester is a reminder of Idaho's heritage as a five car freight from Burley arrives at Rupert on the Eastern Idaho Railroad in 1997. The locomotives are GP30 2228 and SD45 6513 and both started life with the Pennsylvania Railroad.

Right: The Eastern Idaho Railroad was formed in November 1993 when the company took over a cluster of UP branch lines. There are four routes totalling 154 miles in the EIRR's south central segment, based at Twin Falls and Rupert and six routes totalling 116 miles in the south eastern cluster based at Idaho Falls. The company is another owned by Watco Incorporated of Pittsburg, Kansas. At the intermediate depot of Hazelton on the 58 mile Wendell to Rupert branch, this Eastern Idaho pick-up freight will shortly comprise no fewer than 34 freight cars. The red and black locomotives, in this case GP7u 2186 (ex-ATSF) and GP35 786 (ex-UP/WP), have the legend 'The Snake River Route' painted on their bodysides. The grass may be growing long but at least the working railroad survives. This particular line dates back to 1912.

At precisely 19.05 on a very bleak April evening at American Falls Dam in 1997 a pair of UP SD60Ms 6250 and 6101 head a long eastbound rake of empty grain hopper wagons back to the Mid-West, Pocatello being the next major centre of population. The dam across the Snake River is at an elevation of 4,357ft and the original structure was completed in 1927. The present dam dates back to 1978 and the entire railway line had to be raised to accommodate its construction. The derelict former engine house in the foreground would, architecturally, be quite at home in the mining districts of Cornwall in England. Indeed during the mid-1860s there was massive emigration from Cornwall to the Western USA, such was the demand for experienced miners at a time when there was a recession in copper and tin prices and consequently unemployment in the west country of the UK.

It would perhaps be rather trite to describe this photograph as a train snaking along the meandering Snake River but that is exactly what is happening near Glenn's Ferry, Idaho. Evidence has been found of Native American settlements along the river that date back 11,000 years. In more recent times the old Oregon Trail once used by the early pioneers bordered the Snake River in places. The river rises in western Wyoming and it is the longest tributary of the Columbia River, which flows into the Pacific Ocean. With the Sawtooth National Recreation Area in the distant background a mixed train that includes a number of empty lumber cars makes it way towards the Pacific Northwest behind two SD60Ms and an SD60, in the shape of 6177/6023 front and back with 5956 in the middle.

Having traversed much of Idaho this eastbound freight has entered western Wyoming and is seen passing the old mining town of Diamondville, at 6,915ft. The Lincoln County town was incorporated in 1896 and it now has a population of 716. The area is riddled with mining ruins, such as those visible top left. Curving through town on the single track in May 1999 is a typical post merger lash-up of UP C40-8 9342 and a pair of SP SD70Ms. The train will soon be in Green River (see Page 129 et seq). SP's small fleet of 25 SD70M locomotives were mostly used on I-5 corridor trains working out of Roseville.

If you are a 'reefer' fan then this is the train for you. For many years the railways have met the requirements of their customers by providing refrigerated box cars, especially for perishable goods. Looking at the deep snow on the Wasatch Mountains in the background you would think there was enough ice about! Having recently left Idaho this eastbound is negotiating the 90 degree curve at Sage, Wyoming. On the point is C30-7 2486 of 1980 vintage, supported by a rebuilt SP SD45 and UP SD50 5085. Some C30-7s were subsequently rebuilt to a more powerful C36M specification.

Right: It is late April and the Wasatch snows are melting with the run-off flooding the fields at Cokerville, Wyoming. Yet more reefers are on the move out of Idaho but this time behind UP SD60M 6324 and a pair of SD40-2 interlopers from CSX. CSX Transportation Incorporated was formed in July 1986 combining the Seaboard Systems and Chessie System railroad networks. The reason for the appearance of CSX locomotives may have been due to a debit balance of engine hours in favour of UP.

ATSF/BNSF in ARIZONA

The primary ATSF/BNSF rail route across Arizona is hugely varied in every respect but particularly in altitude. From Topock on the California/Arizona border where the altitude is about 500ft to the Arizona Divide between Williams and Flagstaff where a height of 7,313ft is attained, the overall gain of approximate 6,800ft in just over 200 miles changes the topography from desert to mountain forest. The massive railway bridge in the background takes the BNSF across the mighty Colorado River. The river is 1,450 miles long, taking water from the Rocky Mountains of Colorado to the Gulf of California in Mexico and supplying drinking water for 25 million people in the process. The current bridge dates back to 1945. The central pier is 121ft below river level and the bridge can withstand a pressure of 7,200 pounds per linear foot. With the Chemehuevi Mountains in the background a wonderful array of Santa Fe motive power leaves Topock and enters Arizona with over 60 cars (wagons) in tow. Three SD40-2s are assisted by two GP60Ms, in order 5204/5087/153/5100/107, on 4 March 1995, a few months before the merger with BN.

Both Topock and Kingman are located on the old Route 66 but the route between the two towns is circuitous and except for a mile or two the road does not follow the railway. At both locations tacky but fun souvenirs and bric a brac celebrating America's most famous road can be purchased and there is no doubt that the old route with its many closed gas stations and abandoned motels has a certain attraction. Over 158 miles of the old original transcontinental road survive either side of Kingman. Kingman Canyon certainly has attraction as the east and westbound lines split to find a suitable operating gradient. With scenery that would not be out of place in a Hollywood 'Western' a westbound merchandise has an 'elephant style' formation of ATSF C40-8Ws, 870/921/832, on the point as it descends the canyon on 8 May 1996.

North of Kingman the faster freight trains can travel at speeds up to 70mph and Amtrak workings can run at 90mph at certain locations. The double track main line has a high capacity potential and except for engineering windows the route is always busy. There was certainly no point in chasing this double stack train, which is speeding through the Hualapai Valley in a south westerly direction behind 12,000hp of C40-8Ws, this time in the shape of 864/829/842. The early evening light makes the background Peacock Mountains look particularly attractive, not to mention the soon to be abolished Warbonnet livery. The mountains run to a maximum of 5,968ft.

With a trained eye there is always colour to be found in the desert and it is often worth incorporating in a railway photograph. Passing vibrant yellow blooms east of Valentine, a little to the west of Crozier Canyon, a mixed bag of freight wagons are delightfully headed by rebuilt SD45 6414. Behind is a splash of BN Cascade green in the shape of three SD40-2s and a cabless B30-7A 4013. It is now hard to believe but BN once had over 800 SD40-2s on their roster. In the background are the Cottonwood Cliffs and through half closed eyes one can almost see the smoke signals!

Below: Stubbornly failing to recognise the takeovers of the corporate world is this girder bridge over a wash in the heart of Kingman Canyon, however by April 2000 the photographer was fortunate to capture the old Santa Fe livery above the bridge stencil. Heading east are BNSF Dash 9-44CW 4750, LMX Dash 8-39B 8578 and ATSF GP60 8700, albeit with BNSF cab adornment. The westbound line is at a different level, visible towards the base of the photograph.

'Sunset on the Arizona Divide' would be a suitable title for this evocative shot of an eastbound train of pigs passing the 6,000ft mark and nearing the railroad crossing at Maine in May 2003. In the background is the 9,264ft Bill Williams Mountain, which towers above the town of Williams, junction for the Grand Canyon Railroad.

Also starting at Williams is the 1960 built Crookton Cut-off, which was built to avoid the extreme curvature, steep gradients and slow speeds of the old line via Ash Fork, a route now part used only by trains on the Peavine line to Phoenix.

This was the last photograph of the day on 4 May 1998 and what a sight it was. The excitement of being without a scanner and not knowing what may be just around the corner is exemplified by this scene, when the sound of exhaust played on the wind and through the hills for several minutes before the train came into view. One, two, three, four, five ,six, seven, eight went the count as the backlighting highlighted each locomotive. The thunder of their exhausts combined with a reasonable amount of 'clag' being emitted made for a memorable occasion. Swinging through the curves at Hackberry these double stacks are powered by over 30,000hp of diesel electric muscle. For the record the road numbers were 4716/885/852/6308/750/745/GATX 8561/5049.

Winter in Flagstaff, Arizona can be evil as the high altitude and the moist air can produce quite heavy snow falls. High winds can cause the snow to drift giving problems for all types of transportation. Average January daytime highs are 42F and 15F at night. The wettest month is March and the driest is June. Accelerating away from Flagstaff is the eastbound Los Angeles to Chicago 'Southwest Chief', successor to the 'Super Chief'. The 2,256 mile journey will take just over 42 hours. On this day P40s 802 and 811 were in charge as the train departed the depot at 07.35. A railway employee is off to clear the snow from the switches (points).

Right: Christmas card surroundings greet this hot scheduled eastbound intermodal working at Flagstaff. Looking extremely impressive in the morning sunshine is ATSF B40-8W 573 heading four further four axle Warbonnets. The Atlantic & Pacific Railroad arrived in town in 1882, the company eventually being absorbed by the Atchison Topeka & Santa Fe. Up to 60 trains use the route every 24 hours but when linesiding with a camera it never seems quite so busy as the statistics suggest. Note that the station staff have cleared the platform of snow, thereby avoiding possible litigation by falling Amtrak passengers!

In terms of a man versus nature contest the scale of the surrounding topography in northern Arizona would win every time. Against the formidable backdrop of Sheep Hill, near Cosnino, just east of Flagstaff, No 3190 east and two other locomotives heading a long train of triple deck car transporters look diminutive by comparison. The lead GP50 is seen in BNSF Heritage 1 livery, with the roof and body band in 'Pullman Green'. The paint scheme became know as 'Pumpkin' livery. Heritage 2 livery included shaded yellow BNSF lettering, black rather than green colouring and different heraldry on the nose of each cab end.

Below: There is normally little wildlife visible in the badlands, especially in the middle of a hot day in May. It was therefore exceptional to encounter two creatures in such close proximity, with both no doubt looking for a titbit. A healthy looking Raven looks down at a rather sad looking Coyote.

When describing the topography of the wild west it is easy to run out of superlatives but the surroundings at Canyon Diablo are truly awesome. The vast steel structure that bridges the deep crevice of the canyon, seen here on the right, is a whopping 222ft from the ground. The remains of the abutments of an earlier structure can be seen in the centre of the picture. In the left background is the volcanic 12,633ft San Francisco Peak beyond the town of Flagstaff. Dwarfed by the surroundings a six locomotive combination including C40-8CW 924, EMD 6508 and F45 cowl 92 head a long train of box cars, tankers and auto racks, on 5 May 1995. Be warned, the poorly marked dirt track from I-40 to the canyon is hideously bumpy and rocky, not a route for vehicles from Messrs Alamo, Avis, Budget or Hertz!

It is 18.15 on 14 October 1998 and against a quite delightful Arizona sunset the last photograph of the day proved to be the most memorable. As No 4745 west howled through Flagstaff blasting its warning horn in the customary long-long-short-long sequence at crossings, the sun disappeared below the horizon leaving just enough available light to 'have a go' with the camera. The five locomotives on the point of this eastbound intermodal would be given their head once clear of the city limits and its many road crossings. Flagstaff is located in the vast Coconimo County, it sits at an altitude of 6,900ft and the catchment area population is over 45,000. It is the gateway to many National Parks and Indian ruins.

This silhouette of ATSF SD40-2s 5173 and 5009 was taken at sunset at Canyon Diablo on 16 May 1996. The westbound container train had been held 'in the hole' for 40 minutes awaiting a path, a shocking waste of fuel and manpower. The SD40s were (and still are!) remarkable locomotives with 3,858 'straight' Dash 2s being built and when rebuilds are added the total is not far short of 5,000 units. Effectively they were the standard locomotive in the USA during the 1970s and early 1980s, although production of the first 3,000hp SD40 commenced as long ago as 1966.

Left: The BNSF gains access to Phoenix from the north via the 'Peavine Line', a route that diverges from their transcontinental line at Williams. Traditionally the Peavine began at Ash Fork on the pre-Crookton Cut-off main line. The line is difficult to work in terms of the single track, gradients and curvature. Southbound at Congress is 'white face' ex-BN SD40-2 7160 and LMX leaser GE Dash 8-39B 8509 with a light mixed load.

Below left: An old timer slowly passes Kirkland Post Office. Hopefully he is still "hangin' in there".

Below: The Peavine Line dates back to 1894/5 but since that date there have been many track re-alignments. Connections are made at Drake with the Arizona Central Railroad and at Mattie with the Arizona & California Railroad. Traffic on the Peavine is erratic and can vary from between three and six trains per day in each direction but not all during daylight hours. Crossing the short viaduct at Little Hell Canyon this four locomotive consist displays four different livery permutations; BNSF Warbonnet, BNSF Pumpkin, Santa Fe Warbonnet and Santa Fe Bluebonnet. C44-9W 700 leads SD40-2 6795, GP60M 135 and SD45-2 6470 southbound on 15 October 1998.

ACROSS WYOMING

Overlooked by the dramatically named Flaming Gorge National Recreation Area eastbound reefers hit the curve at Rock Springs, Wyoming with an interesting combo up front. UP C40-8 No 9292 leads Norfolk Southern C30-7 No 8079 (ex-Norfolk & Western) and Conrail SD60 No 5598. The last two locomotives are probably balancing engine horsepower hours with UP. The train is adopting the common North American practise of right hand running on double track whereas in many other countries, including the United Kingdom, left had running is the norm. However just to throw a spanner in the works many modern lines are bi-directional sending time honoured convention to the wall.

Classic Sherman Hill country is illustrated here, where once upon a time the largest steam locomotives in the land hauled massive loads up fierce gradients. Slaving up the last few yards to the Hermosa Tunnels, which comprise two single bores, is UP 9330 east with what appear to be soda ash hopper wagons. These C40-8 locomotives were produced between 1987 and 1991 and were some of the last produced without full width comfort cabs. Although the lead locomotive has air conditioning the superior modern full width cab package was not introduced until 1989.

Right: Anyone for the barbecue? Prior to taking this photograph there had been plumes of black smoke rising above UP's Green River depot and one suspected that somebody was burning a load of old car tires (tyres). It never occurred that there could be a locomotive problem until this westbound rounded the curve. With flames leaping up to 20ft into the air UP C40-8 wide cab 9369 clearly has an exhaust fire, possibly caused by the ignition of diesel fuel that had not combusted in the normal way. The train continued on its merry way possibly because UP 9368 and CNW 5075 were doing all the work or more likely because the engineer was oblivious to events above the roofline. Either visuals or instruments would soon tell him otherwise. Note the magnificent Castle Rock in the background (there are several Castle Rocks in the west).

Wyoming became a newly formed State in 1891. As early as the 1860s the railway builders realised that crossing the territory by rail presented a significant problem, due to the formidable altitude and the implied gradients that would be necessary for trains to reach such heights. The original Sherman Hill summit was 8,247ft but 1901 track re-alignments reduced this to 8,013ft. This westbound intermodal with UP 9220 leading is seen approaching the Hermosa Tunnels from the east but unlike some high altitude railroads there are no tunnels at the actual summit, a point on the map that this train has already passed. Wooden snow fences line the right of way in this area.

Below left: There are some small towns in Wyoming and in many other parts of the wild west but it would be difficult to find a smaller population than that of Buford. If a couple had twins the population would double overnight or if they went out for the evening it would become a ghost town!

The UP main line across Wyoming is extremely busy and over the years it has been necessary to increase capacity over Sherman Hill, where the slowest and heaviest trains run at low average speeds. Accordingly additional tracks have been provided on both the Laramie and Cheyenne sides of the hill. Half a dozen maps would be necessary to show every change. For example in 1952 the 'Harriman Cut-off' from Cheyenne to Dale Junction was opened reducing gradients considerably. Also in recent years there has been a four track section out of Cheyenne. There are also different speed limits on different lines, which vary from 40mph to 60mph. Climbing from Laramie to the Sherman Hill summit are two UP owned CNW liveried C44-9s, 8663 and 8637, photographed near Perkins in May 1999.

Cheyenne is a major UP installation with a variety of yards, facilities and infrastructure. In the days of steam the motive power depot was legendary and housed many of the largest locomotives in the world, including the famous 'Big Boys'. A well known afternoon 'phot-spot' in downtown Cheyenne is where the old Colorado & Southern Railroad (later BN and now BNSF) crosses the UP main line. The silver bridge has been darkened by westbound exhaust gasses, a situation that will not be helped by UP SD9043MAC 8168 west and a sister locomotives as they hit the 0.82 per cent grade with coal hoppers.

THE SUNSET ROUTE

It's a long haul from Los Angeles to El Paso but Collis Huntington of Central Pacific/Southern Pacific fame saw the value of such a rail route. Construction started at Los Angeles in 1877, reaching Tucson in 1880 and El Paso, 760 miles away, in 1881. The route was via West Colton, San Timoteo Canyon, Palm Springs, Beaumont, Acolita, Yuma, Shawmut, Casa Grande, Tucson, Cochise to El Paso (and from February 1883, after a number acquisitions, New Orleans). In Victorian times the line became known as the Sunset Route and a setting sun over a tapering railway track became the SP's logo and trademark. On 1 April 1996 eastbound double stacks were photographed at Hinda, near Beaumont, between San Bernardino and Palm Springs, headed by two SP SD40T-2s, a B40-8 and two GP60s; 8324/5412/8077/9725 and (DRGW) 3154. The route is noted for its lack of tunnels, which facilitated double stack operations in the 1980s.

It now seems inconceivable that as a late middle aged lone traveller one would drive a hire car on a 25 mile round trip on a dirt road, climb this perilous hill avoiding rocks and critters and stand in the heat for five hours simply to photograph a train or two. However in retrospect and in viewing the resulting imagery from an armchair 15 years after the event, it was all worth it. With a symbolic Saguaro cacti in the foreground and with the Maricopa Mountains behind a westbound SP container train headed by a pair of GE C44-9s passes Shawmut, east of Gila Bend. Note that the east and westbound tracks briefly separate at this point.

Below: Some of the magnificent Saguaro cacti develop almost human forms, even if in this case the plant has four arms and two noses! Strangely the cacti are not found in Texas, New Mexico, Colorado or Nevada, being native to Arizona and part of Mexico. This example would be at least 100 years old.

Death eventually stretches its arm to every living thing and the proud Saguaro cacti is no exception. A native of the Sonoran Desert the Saguaro can grow to a height of 45ft with a girth of 10ft and examples can live for up to 150 years. The plant is pollinated by bats. However this poor old cacti has had its day and its main structural ribs have been exposed. These were sought after by Native Americans and used in building construction. Burning across the desert at Shawmut at 08.37 on 2 October 1998 is an underpowered UP double stack train behind a trio of SD40-2s. Standing out in the background are the Sauceda Mountains. A former tightly curved and now abandoned track alignment can be seen on the left.

Yuma is one of the sunniest places in the wild west. On average 90 per cent of all the days in the year are sunny. There is only three inches of rain per annum and in the wettest month of August there is just 0.61in of precipitation. In August the average day time high is 106F cooling off at night to 80F. At this time of the evening the headlights and ditchlights of an SD40-2 are stronger than the available daylight giving a slightly unusual effect. With the Gila Mountains behind westbound double stacks headed by UP SD40-2s 3464 and 3703 lead C30-7 2477 and rebuilt SP liveried GP40 7281 pass Blaisdell, a few miles east of Yuma.

One of the problems with the Sunset Route is the amount of single track mileage. When UP took over the SP in 1996 less than a quarter of the route was double track. Since then they have spent $105m installing 169 miles of additional double track. Upgrading the route is important because forecasters are predicting that trade between the US and Asia will double by 2020. Amtrak's 'Sunset Limited' traverses the route but delays caused by long single track sections resulted in Amtrak once taking SP to court seeking compensation for delays. The 'Sunset Limited' is the oldest named train in the USA still running, having commenced service back in 1894, although since hurricane Katrina the express has terminated in New Orleans rather than Florida. Presently there are three trains per week in each direction. On 8 May 1995 SD40T-2 5354 west passes Picacho, junction for the Phoenix line (seen on the left) with westbound containers. In the right background is Picacho Peak, height 3,374ft.

GATEWAY to OREGON

Gateway *from* Oregon would be a more appropriate title for this photograph taken at Dorris south of Klamath Falls. The small Californian town of Dorris has a population of 886, it sits at an altitude of 4,245ft and it boasts a railway tunnel, Tunnel #17, on the former SP Shasta Line. Also heading south from Klamath Falls are the BNSF 'Highline' to Bieber and Keddie and the short stub of the old SP Madoc line to northern Nevada, which closed as a through route in 1987 after traffic had dwindled to one train per day in each direction. Approaching Tunnel #17 in May 2007 is UP ES44AC 5329 plus two other UP and two BNSF locomotives, with a southbound freight for Dunsmuir and beyond. The UP winged shield was re-introduced on UP locomotive cab ends from April 2000.

Right: Many will say "those were the days" when most Oregon lumber branch lines were still open and espee SD9Es still ruled the roost. Local trains worked out of Medford to White City, Grants Pass and Ashland but sadly the main north to south Siskiyou through route was finally closed by the Central Oregon Pacific Railroad in 2008. The line was closed for nearly 18 months in 2003/5 due to a serious fire in Tunnel #13. The Siskiyou line was difficult to operate with tight curves, a maximum 3.1 per cent grade and an annual maintenance bill of $7,000 per mile over the 81 mile route. The tunnels were too low for double stacks or auto racks. Right beside Medford depot Nos 4402/4314/4333 pause between duties in July 1991.

Below: The main gateway into Oregon from the east is along the Columbia River, which has already been described in a previous section. However so important is the artery that this conventional shot of an immaculate repainted SD50, which was withdrawn from UP service over a decade ago, just had to be included. But for the repaint this would have been an all-CNW lash-up because No 5090 had been inherited from the 1995 takeover of the Chicago company and the two CNW C44-9 sisters, No 8664 and 8648, still carried CNW colours. The trio are hauling a substantial consist of auto racks at Covert's Landing, near Wyeth, Oregon.

Right: Over the years there have been a huge number of branch lines in Oregon that only the local expert could track. Wonderful books such as Bob Leachman's 'North West Passage' and Brian Jennison's and Victor Neeves' 'Southern Pacific Oregon Division' deal with the subject comprehensively. The Sweet Home branch, south east of Albany, started life as the Oregon Electric Railway but for decades it was BN territory. The line served lumber mills and sidings at Lebanon and Sweet Home, as well as intermediate sites such as Bauman Lumber. In May 1998 the Albany & Eastern Railroad leased the branch from BNSF. The branch joins the Willamette Valley Railroad to Mill City at Lebanon. On 12 September 1997, when BN still ruled the roost, GP38-2 2266 is seen returning from Sweet Home with two lumber cars and a caboose, as a hint of autumn colour appears in the surrounding foliage.

The Oregon Trunk route through the spectacular Deschutes Canyon is a fabulous piece of railway track, which has become a personal favourite. The main problem is the paucity of traffic where a whole day of a costly vacation can easily be spent tracking down and photographing just one train in each direction. The line from Wishram on the Columbia River to Bend opened in 1909 in the pursuit of the ambitions of James J Hill, who was known as the 'Empire Builder'. However it would be 1931 before the last spike was driven into the track at Bieber, California giving through access to Keddie on the Feather River Route via the 'Highline', thereby completing what became known as the 'Inside Gateway'. Three of BN's 800-odd SD40-2s, 6835/8051/7835, head KCS SD50 753 and a westbound merchandise train (geographically heading north) across the viaduct over the Deschutes River on the approach to Tunnel #2 on 15 September 1997.

The Oregon Trunk route is steeply graded, for example the climb up onto the Oregon Plateau calls for 20 miles at 1.5 per cent and from Bend to Klamath the ruling gradient is 1.3 per cent. There are also some truly spectacular viaducts on the way, across the Crooked River, Trout Creek and also at Madras. Crossing the rapids, this southbound freight runs high above the Deschutes River and is about to plunge into Tunnel #2 behind BN SD40-2 7071, Montana Rail Link SD45 361 (formerly Susquehanna 3632) and BN C30-7 5018. The first two cars remain in Great Northern livery, GN being one of four companies that merged into Burlington Northern 26 years earlier, in 1971.

THE CASCADE MOUNTAINS

Excluding the Columbia River there are three other major railroad crossings of the Cascade Mountains. In Washington State the most northerly route is from Everett to Wenatchee via Cascade Tunnel and further south is the Stampede Pass route from Auburn to Yakima. In Oregon the primary crossing is from Eugene to Chemult via the Cascade Loops. An early breakfast was worthwhile on 9 September 1997 when at 07.32 the headlights of the westbound 'Empire Builder' pierced the dense fog at Gold Bar, Washington. AMTK P40 816 plus a sister locomotive have averaged 50mph on their 2,206 mile run with the Chicago to Seattle portion of the train. A Portland, Oregon section was split from the train at Spokane, although this was not the case from 1971 to 1981. Some half million passengers per annum use this flagship of the old Great Northern Railway (GNR).

The Cascades and the Pacific Northwest can be very, very wet but to exclude such scenes from a pictorial survey of the wild west would be unrepresentative. It is pouring down at Baring, Washington - population 233, but the trains are still running, including these westbound wood chips. Tip toeing their way off the Stevens Pass route across the Cascades are BNSF 7088/7928/6926/4061 as they pass Mountain View general store. It was too cold and wet to be tempted inside for some 'party ice' or the advertised 'Millers Genuine Draft' beer.

This and the following photograph have been deliberately paired to show the dramatic difference in climatic conditions that can be experienced at the same location in the mighty Cascade range. The mountains run in a north to south direction and extend for over 600 miles, from British Columbia to Northern California. Famous peaks include Mount Ranier, Baker, St Helens, Hood and Shasta, some of which are similar to the Swiss Alps in altitude. For example the peak of Mount Shasta is at 14,162ft and is snow covered all year round. With low cloud swirling between the foothills westbound double stacks cross the North Fork of the Skykomish River at Index while in the process of negotiating a 180 degree curve. Providing the head end power are BN 7823/6372/(ATSF SD45-2) 5830/3104, shortly after the BN/ATSF merger.

Although the photographs within these pages reflect the changeover from second to third generation motive power the news in 2010 was that both UP and BNSF were planning to put several hundred of their secondary locomotive fleets through works. Between them this would include over 500 EMD SD40-2s, which would be overhauled under 'life extension' programmes with upgrades in their emission ratings to comply with current legislation and, where relevant, by fitting microprocessor control systems. Although the locomotives would mainly be confined to local and yard duties these venerable machines are likely to be part of the railroad scene for many years to come.

Following the 2008/9 recession thousands of locomotives were stored throughout the USA and Canada. The years 2009/10 were a disaster for locomotive manufacturers and leasing companies resulting in staff lay-offs. As a consequence and to the surprise of many both UP and BNSF pensioned off significant numbers of GE Dash 8-40CWs, with CN acquiring over 60 of these locomotives from the US Class 1 operators. Later in the year there was some commercial improvement and on the plus side GE's 'Evolution' series in both d.c. and a.c. configurations sold well and a new A1A-A1A version was being tested by BNSF. In addition to their SD70 range, again in d.c. and a.c. modes, EMD/Caterpillar were offering their EMD710ECO two stroke diesel to re-engine a range of older models. With products from Motive Power/Watco , National Railway Equipment/Genset and others making an impact on the market it is clear that the motive power scene in the wild west will continue to be ever varied and ever evolving.

It is 08.25 and the sun has just risen above the Cascade range providing a truly stunning vista at Index, with remarkable visibility. The small town is located adjacent to this old GNR route and at an elevation of only 577ft the 159 residents will not get snowed-in as often as their uphill neighbours. Nearby is the 5,979ft Mount Index. Crossing a single span bridge across the North Fork of the Skykomish River on this wonderful autumn morning with eastbound containers are BNSF C44-9W 722, ATSF GP50 3846, and unsurprisingly a trio of BN/BNSF SD40-2s 7856/6915/6700. The train will soon be climbing against a 1.57 per cent ruling gradient up to Cascade Tunnel.

After a 3 hour wait a train finally emerged from the western portal of Cascade Tunnel on 9 September 1997. At 7.79 miles the bore is the longest through tunnel in the USA, although with a 2,881ft east end elevation, it is far from the highest. This is the second Cascade Tunnel, two earlier and higher routes being abandoned in 1928/9. Officially known as Tunnel #15 the lengthy bore requires a dedicated ventilation plant to help clear exhaust gases. BN 7170 was on the point of a westbound double stack working and being a dead straight bore its headlights were visible for ages as it crossed the Cascades. Evidence in the foreground suggests a rail replacement programme is in progress.

Right: In Oregon the Eugene to Chemult 'Pengra Pass' route across the mountains involves a 90 mile climb to the 4,839ft Cascade summit. In 1952 a revised 22 mile track alignment was built at the Eugene end because of new reservoir construction. The remarkable line has 29 tunnels and numerous snow sheds, plus a formidable piece of trackwork called the 'Cascade Loops'. At the higher elevations much of the line is inaccessible except for the most athletic or foolhardy enthusiasts. A popular spot for photography, although rapidly becoming overgrown, is Salt Creek Trestle (one of several in the west) near a location known as Heather. A westbound merchandise crosses the 515ft long structure headed by visiting Conrail SD60I 5601 and supported by UP SD50 5038, CNW GP40 5525 and UP SD40-2 3292. The Conrail locomotive was assembled at the company's Juniata shops from a kit supplied by EMD. In January 2008 a massive landslide on Coyote Mountain destroyed 1,600ft of track, which was under 20ft of mud and trees. The line was closed for over 2 months.

The Pengra Pass route, known as the 'Natron Cut-off', was a relatively late arrival not being ready for service until September 1926, although there was plenty of other railroad building in the area before the through route was opened. The maximum grade on the route is a steep 2.2 per cent. There are approximately 15 trains per day over the line including most of the longer distance I-5 corridor traffic that runs from Roseville to Portland via Klamath Falls, one train running from Eugene to West Colton. The opportunity to capture on film an all SP consist after the takeover by UP was thankfully accepted. This little piece of history shows SP speedletter livery applied to both SD70Ms 9816 and 9817 with convention being retained in respect of supporting SP tunnel motor 8245. The intermodal train is seen descending near Heather, the train having just successfully negotiated the Cascade Loops. The idea behind the procurement of the SD70Ms was to move the lucrative Pacific Northwest timber traffic using two powerful high adhesion locomotives with steerable trucks instead of four second generation tunnel motors. (See page 25 for comments on the Stampede Pass route over the Cascades).

DONNER PASS

In terms of locomotives and liveries this May 2007 shot takes us to the end of our time frame in 'Railroading in the Wild West'. Sporting what has been called 'Swoosh' livery, first introduced in 2005 when the 'Heritage' paint schemes were discontinued, is low emission BNSF ES44DC 7774, which with a pair Dash 9-44CWs is rolling down the hill into Colfax in Placer County, California with a mixed load. The town with 1,496 inhabitants is named after US Vice President Schuyler Colfax who visited the settlement in 1865 to check on progress with the Central Pacific Railroad. Colfax has a station and is served by Amtrak's 'California Zephyr' (see Page 69). The Donner Pass route took 5 years to build, largely by Chinese labour, over some of the most hostile terrain imaginable. Opened in June 1868 the line broadly followed the route of the old wagon trains but with a liberal sprinkling of tunnels, viaducts and snow sheds. The CP route became SP property for most of its life until the UP takeover in 1996.

This conventional but classic consist is typical of the SP pre-merger days on Donner Pass. Sporting the 1991 speedlettering (an influence of the Phil Anschultz/D&RGW takeover) on its time-honoured red and grey livery, SD45T-2 9273 leads no fewer than six SD40 and SD40T dash-2 locomotives in the shape of 6882/7305/7359/8258/6857/6866, near Colfax on their descent of the Sierras with a wonderfully mixed westbound freight for Roseville. UP have made a considerable investment in the line, enlarging 15 tunnels to accept 22ft tall double stacks and 20ft 2in auto racks, saving a 3 hour journey time compared with the alternative Feather River Route. The modifications that included 18,000 linear feet of 'notching', lowering the floors of two tunnels and fitting 'rock bolts' for stability to another five tunnels, were ready for service on 19 November 2009.

Below: This coyote warning has been posted on top of a bear warning, both potential problems in mountainous regions. Many US citizens are keen campers who in conservation areas and National Parks in particular adhere to a code of practise, relating to everything from food storage at camp sites to starting fires in the wilderness at certain times of year or in dry climatic conditions.

AREA CLOSED TO FOOD OUTSIDE OF VEHICLES DUE TO AGGRESSIVE COYOTE

Contact Lake Ranger Station at (307) 242-2401 if animal is seen

Left: Rugged is the adjective that comes to mind when viewing this scene in the Sierras. The location is at Yuba Pass, just off of Highway I-80 from Sacramento to Reno and Salt Lake City, and against this attractive backdrop the westbound 'California Zephyr' is seen leaving Tunnel #35 behind F40PHs 380 and 300. These cowl locomotives packed an EMD 645E punch of 3,200hp but they were only 56ft 2in long. On their journey passengers will see Reno, Truckee, Soda Springs, Donner Lake, Crystal Lake, Yuba Pass, Emigrant Gap, Dutch Flat, Gold Run, Colfax, Auburn and a whole lot more. Over the years there have been many track deviations over Donner Pass. In the early days tracks were added, with much doubling work being undertaken in 1925, but more recently there has been considerable rationalisation, such as the removal of 6.7 miles of the old Track 1 in 1993. The previous location of the former second track can be seen here, which no doubt gives the train dispatchers headaches at times.

Right: It was a pleasant surprise to see these old SP girls in action at Truckee on 10 September 1994. Although Nos 4366 and 4412 had been rebuilt to SD9E specification in 1973 and 1976 respectively they dated back to the 1955 and 1956 period, which meant that their primary structures were already nearly 40 years of age. By this time the locomotives had been relegated to mundane duties and the pair were toying with a couple of engineers wagons when photographed. The SP ordered 149 of these units and with the demise of passenger trains 50 subsequently had their steam generators removed and fuel capacity increased, following water tank removal.

Right: In the days of 'espee' operations on the Donner Pass route a long westbound grain train is seen descending through Soda Springs. The train has just passed the summit at Norden at an altitude of just over 7,000ft. The climate is not always as kind as on this day and in the winter snow falls can be heavy. In 1952 a passenger train was stuck in a snow drift for 6 days before it could be rescued. The whine of the dynamics will soon be audible as a pair of SP SD40T-2 tunnel motors head down the hill, with 8318 leading, plus a pair of venerable SD45s, all of them in typical SP external condition. Some blamed the tunnels rather than the maintenance schedules for the discolouration!

CANYONS and DESERTS

If an artist had painted this scene there is little doubt that viewers would have said that the colours were 'all wrong'. This is Afton Canyon, California, a site of immense historical, geological, zoological and of course railway interest. The canyon was created only about 18,000 years ago as a result of a massive flood and even today water is a feature in that it is one of the few places where the Mojave River flows above ground. The UP track through the canyon is single and there are three steel bridges on its twisting course, this two section example being at milepost 196.12. The altitude is 1,640ft. The sight of long multi-headed freights becomes so commonplace in this area that a single locomotive and just four wagons makes for a novel sight on a Class 1 railroad. UP C40-8 9149 makes for Yermo and Barstow, which is just 37 miles away.

Here we see another kaleidoscope of colour in Afton Canyon. It really is a very special place and a visit is highly recommended. Unfortunately there are some pitfalls in that although the author has accessed the canyon from both an easterly and a westerly direction there has been some risk attached in testing the depth of water in the Mojave River and its 'puddles'. If the car stalled due to damp electrics the traveller would have a very significant problem in this remote area. At 09.53 on 4 April 1996 a westbound coal drag from Utah threads the canyon behind UP SD40-2s 3128/3253/3480 and, second in line, a dusty C41-8W 9542. On this day there were 3 westbound and 2 eastbound freights in a period of 4 hours with the longest gap being 1 hour and 40 minutes.

The words 'hot-shot' are sometimes casually used but on occasions the nature of the train and the power made available leads one to the logical and perhaps inevitable conclusion that a train is on a fast schedule. This was certainly the case in May 2007 when heavyweight super power of no less than four UP SD70ACs and two further locomotives headed a westbound double stacker through Kelso. No 8337 west looks impressive in the late afternoon light with the Providence Mountains as a backdrop. The photograph was taken from the handsome railway depot at Kelso that was built in 1923 with Californian Mission style architecture. It closed in 1986 but following refurbishment it reopened as the Mojave National Preserve visitor centre. Nearby are the impressive Kelso sand dunes that rise 650ft from the desert floor and are home to the Giant Sand Treader cricket and the Mojave Fringe-toed Lizard, which 'swims' under the sand.

Inset: The Mojave Tortoise is a threatened species and should not be handled or harassed. They have many predators including ravens, gila monsters, foxes, badgers, roadrunners, coyotes, fire ants and above all man. Those that survive live for between 80 and 100 years. They grow to between 10 and 14 inches, weigh 8 to 15 pounds and spend 95 per cent of their time underground. They can survive for up to 12 months without water, although they extract moisture from the plants they eat. Over the years the author has seen three examples near the lineside, this one at Nipton.

Below right: This plaque is located at Nipton, showing the railway origins of the town, as provided by the E Clampus Vitus organisation. This Ancient and Honourable Order does a tremendous job in studying and preserving western heritage and provides historical markers at interesting sites throughout the wild west.

NIPTON

THE TOWN OF NIPTON WAS BORN ON FEBRUARY 9, 1905 WITH THE COMING OF THE FIRST TRAIN ON THE NEWLY CONSTRUCTED SAN PEDRO, LOS ANGELES AND SALT LAKE RAILROAD. ORIGINALLY CALLED NIPPENO CAMP AFTER A NEARBY GOLD DISCOVERY, THE NAME WAS CHANGED TO NIPTON WHEN THE SP, LA & SL MERGED WITH THE UNION PACIFIC CIRCA 1910. FOR MANY YEARS, THE DEPOT WAS A CATTLE-LOADING STATION FOR SEVERAL LOCAL RANCHES INCLUDING YATES RANCH, THE WALKING BOX, AND ROCK SPRINGS LAND AND CATTLE CO. THE TOWN AND DEPOT ALSO SUPPLIED NUMEROUS MINES IN THE AREA, BECOMING A SOCIAL CENTER FOR THE SPARSE POPULATION OF THE REGION. COMMUNITY FACILITIES INCLUDED A SCHOOL, POST OFFICE, VOTER PRECINCT, AND SEVERAL SMALL BUSINESSES. BEGUN AS A 20TH CENTURY RAILROAD DEPOT, NIPTON IS RE-FORMING INTO A 21ST CENTURY GATEWAY TO THE MOJAVE NATIONAL PRESERVE.

Plaque placed October 10, 1999 by Billy Holcomb Chapter and Queho Posse of the Ancient and Honorable Order of E Clampus Vitus.

As the suns dips across the Ivanpah Valley emphasising the folds in the bare distant hills a now abandoned Amtrak working rattles along the iron road at Nipton. It now seems hard to believe that there is no regular passenger service between Los Angeles and Las Vegas but the 'Desert Wind' was axed on 12 May 1997, having had a life of only 18 years. A year before withdrawal F40PHs 388 and 292 roll off Cima Hill bound for Salt Lake City where some of these coaches will be added to the 'California Zephyr' that will end up in Chicago. Nipton is a wonderful desert oasis with a small hotel, general store and bar. It owes its origin to the railroad, which arrived in 1905, and local mining activities.

Above: Further along the valley beyond Roach dry lake and the resort of Primm is the settlement of Jean, Nevada. Two great casino/hotels were built either side of I-15 (one of them, Nevada Landing, has since been demolished), together with gas stations, a post office, court house and correctional institution. About 7 miles to the west is the old mining town of Goodsprings where the local school and the old Pioneer Saloon, both dating back to about 1913, continue to operate. The town was once served by a narrow gauge mining railroad, linked to the Yellow Pine Mine. In January 1942 the Hollywood actor Clark Gable reputedly drank in the Pioneer while waiting for news about the air crash that killed the love of his life, actress Carol Lombard. The TWA Douglas DC3 she was travelling in crashed nearby on the 8,504ft Mount Potosi, killing all 22 aboard. The local JP is Dawn Haviland who has the power to marry you or jail you and is clearly somebody to befriend, which I have!

Right: In this 'association of ideas' shot from the barred window of the 10th floor of the Gold Strike desert casino and hotel at Jean, Nevada the local prison can be seen in the centre of the frame. The all female establishment is more accurately called a minimum security Conservation Camp by the Department of Correction. Passing the camp is an eastbound container train with three road units on the point. Personally I would prefer to view the passing trains from behind these bars!

This is not a location to be visited by those suffering from claustrophobia or a vivid imagination. The ghosts of times past and a snake or two may live in old Tunnel #2 at Sloan, Nevada, just east of Eire summit, but otherwise it is eerily silent until a train approaches when the sound of the exhaust, the wail of a warning horn and the clatter of the wheels echo throughout the disused tunnel. The tunnel was abandoned in 1943 when it was bypassed by a new alignment in a deep cutting. Over the years some quite substantial rocks have fallen from the roof of the tunnel but thankfully not on this day! An eastbound merchandise train passes, headed by an UP SD60.

The old Los Angeles and Salt Lake, now Union Pacific, route is no racing ground. In fact 280 of the 785 miles are speed restricted to 45mph or less. Nevertheless it is a main artery and during a 24 hour period there can be up to 10 freights in each direction. Traffic is expected to increase as the ports of Los Angeles and Long Beach do more and more trade with Pacific Rim countries. With a blaze of colour in the foreground an eastbound mixed manifest curves around Sloan on 2 May 1998 behind fore and aft UP SD60Ms 6218 and 6299, with a SP SD45 rebuild in the middle. Note that even by 10.50 the sun is so high that the lighting on the train, even on a sunny day, is poor in terms of photography.

Below: During the summer months one has to feel almost sorry for the diesel locomotives working hard across the desert terrain, where the air temperatures are often well into three figures. Despite cooling systems their temperature gauges must be 'knocking on the red' on occasions. Over the years significant improvements in the driving cabs have been made including wide cabs, isolated cabs, whisper cabs and above all sophisticated air conditioning systems – all far removed from the fiery footplate of a steam engine. This eastbound at Sloan is enjoying a 17 mile 1 per cent downhill rest as it makes for Las Vegas in April 2000. The machinery is UP C41-8W 9505, CNW SD60 8012 and good old UP SD40-2 3345.

There are 40 to 50 species of the Yucca plant. It has tough sword shaped leaves, whitish flowers and it thrives in rocky deserts and badlands with a hot and dry climate. They can be found in large numbers between Afton and Clover Creek Canyons, the 'length' of this chapter. This Wasco to Provo train of coal empties is only yards away from reaching the top of the gruelling 2.2 per cent climb from Kelso to Cima on 2 May 1998. In this post-takeover view it was very satisfying to find two Southern Pacific liveried GE AC44CWs 282 and 147, on the point as they passed the west switch. Some of these locomotives retained SP colours until 2004. UP C44/60CW 7028 is in support. There are interesting lava cones in the area and the remains of a few old miners shacks.

Right: You won't find any lumberjacks in this part of Nevada! The only wood in sight in this arid and desolate scene is the line of spindly telegraph poles on the hillside. This very impressive American President Lines double stack container train is 19 miles from Las Vegas and it has been climbing at a steady 1 per cent for the entire distance. There is absolutely nothing but desert in sight as UP SD40-2 3722 and four other units climb towards Eire summit, thereafter having a breather on the downhill dash into the Ivanpah Valley. There was still plenty of this westbound train to come from behind the photographer and the entire consist would soon be crossing the track alignment just visible at the top of the picture.

While it is encouraging to find industry in the desert, bringing with it welcome employment, this is not a plant that you would want for an immediate neighbour. It is the Nevada Power Company's Reid Gardner Power Station at Moapa. It is located 60 miles north east of Las Vegas. Opened in stages between 1965 and 1983 it is a 4 unit 650mv coal fired plant. Hopefully conditions have since improved but according to the Environmental Integrity Project report it was, in terms of emissions, once the nation's dirtiest coal fired power generator in the USA, in the process using 1.9 million tons of coal per annum. Even the local Paiute tribe complained about the smell from the plant. However in terms of industrial aesthetics it makes a great backcloth for a railroad shot, as UP SD40-2s 3761/3460/3390 reverse into the works with hopper wagons in May 2003.

Unless you are a mountaineer or at least an expert hiker the only way into Clover Creek Canyon is along the UP service road, just visible bottom left. Even a decade ago a well behaved interloper would not have been challenged, especially if offering a friendly wave to the train crew. However things have changed since the morally reprehensible '9/11' atrocity and now a visitor would be regarded as either a trespasser or even a terrorist, which is a shame. In the most wonderful surroundings and on a perfect day in Clover Creek Canyon eastbound stacks round the curve at Islen behind UP 9456/6341/6355 and CNW 8701. The main danger here is the large mosquitoes that breed in the many puddles along the creek!

This pair of UP GE C40-8s simply exude power as they thunder eastward past the depot at Caliente (not to be confused with Caliente, California on Tehachapi) in the very early morning light on 16 April 1997, no doubt waking some of the residents and visitors. Located at 4,300ft Caliente was once a quite large town with a population of over 5,000 but as the mines closed and the area contracted commercially this has now reduced to a mere 1,000. The splendid mission style 1922 built railway depot building still stands and is well worth a visit, especially as trains regularly pass through town. The old depot had previously burnt to the ground. There are plenty of motels and diners and Caliente is a great place to stay if photographing in either the Meadow Valley Wash, Clover Creek Canyon, or surrounding areas.

At the other end of the day the shadows are growing long in Clover Creek Canyon, a mile or two from Islen. Passing milepost 477 and producing a backlit glint is a westbound freight headed by UP SD60 No 6018. The train would soon be in Caliente. The railway heavily influenced the town and it once boasted a 20 stall roundhouse, turntable, a substantial yard and even dedicated railway employee houses. It was also the junction for a branch line to Pioche, which was finally abandoned in 1984. Modernisation and dieselisation in the late 1940s was to be the death knell of the town in terms of railway importance. For those interest in a detailed account of the route Mark Hemphill's book 'Union Pacific Salt Lake Route' is highly recommended.

You have to be either fit, brave or foolhardy to reach this incredibly remote but awe inspiring photographic vantage point between Hoya and Galt in the heart of Huntsman Canyon. Situated about 70 miles north of Las Vegas and 55 miles south of Caliente there is not a living soul to be seen in this inhospitable area, except for passing train crews. The area is very susceptible to flash floods and in the past the railroad has been washed-out many times, the last occasion, albeit a little further north, being in January 2005. In fact the old rail route was once at a lower level, the trackbed being just visible on the far left, beyond the service road. Threading the rocks is an eastbound merchandise (travelling north!) hauled by UP C30-7 2461, SD40-2s 3933 and 3685 and SP tunnel motor 8325.

One of the joys of exploring these off the beaten track locations in pursuit of railway photography is simply 'poking around' some of the backwaters. This is the old Mormon settlement of Barclay in the Clover Valley, about a dozen miles east of Caliente, accessible down a lengthy and undulating dirt road. The hamlet comprises a couple of ranches, a couple of old dwellings, a pioneer cemetery and this old 1898 single room schoolhouse. Surprisingly it has since been refurbished, painted white and fenced! The last child has long since departed as former CNW C44-9 8702 and UP 6347 and 3837 rush by with westbound containers under a partially cloudy sky.

FRASER RIVER CANYON

The Fraser River Canyon is a major transport artery between the Rocky Mountains and the Canadian Pacific Coast. It is not only the river that flows through the canyon but also the Trans-Canadian highway and both the Canadian National Railway and the Canadian Pacific Railway, now CN and CP Rail. The CPR completed their transcontinental railway line in 1885 although activity in the canyon reached fever pitch years before, in 1858, when gold was discovered, leading to a predictable gold rush. A further gold rush in the Cariboo region followed in 1864. By that date it is estimated that 10,000 miners were in the canyon north of Yale. The scale of the surroundings is evident in this view of CP Rail 5860 west on a merchandise train on 14 October 1991. The train has four of CP Rail's (nearly) 500 examples of the SD40-2 class on the point.

Right: It is not only US railroads that have their spectacular trestles. This is CN's Anderson Creek Trestle near Boston Bar, an old mining town. The creek runs down the hillside to meet the Fraser River in the canyon below. This eastbound freight has empty grain cars to the fore. Head end power is provided by CN SD50 cowl unit 5427 followed by the evergreen SD40s 5266 and 5379, although the former example is of the SD40-2W variety. In 2000 there was a proposal for a BNSF/CN merger but this was diluted to 'closer working partnership' status. In the early days British Columbia, the most western of the Canadian Provinces, thrived on three major industries, fishing, forestry and farming, the latter including the fur and pelt trade originally promoted by the Hudson Bay Company.

Glorious autumn tints are appearing on the mountainsides bordering the Fraser River, which makes the CN train look almost insignificant compared with the wonders of nature. Running along its single track ledge is a grain train from the Canadian Prairies bound for Vancouver but whether the content of the wagons is for export or internal consumption is anybody's guess. CN have mated a SD60F 5563 with SD50F

5449, seen near Hell's Gate where a 'SkyTram' aerial cableway takes passengers in a gondola car on a hair-raising ride over the gorge. You will need to have a C$20 bill with you but you should be able to buy a coffee with the change. The mandatory gift shop, restaurants, museum and 'facilities' are provided and you might see a train or two on the way across.

For almost the entire distance from New Westminster to Yale and Spuzzam the CN tracks run on the southern and eastern side of the Fraser River and CP Rail operates on the northern and western side. However further up the canyon towards Lytton, nearer to the confluence of the Thompson and Fraser Rivers, the railways cross each other, adding to the geographical confusion. With the mountains developing a blue hue in the late afternoon light, CP Rail SD40-2s 5931 and 6019 are seen north of Yale with empty hopper wagons. The twin signals show that the train is at a bi-directional passing siding (loop).

One of the more successful tourist operations in British Columbia and Alberta has been the 'Rocky Mountaineer'. The special trains run over four routes with the primary objective of giving passengers the best possible view of the magnificent scenery between Vancouver and the Rocky Mountains, mainly to Calgary via Banff and also to Jasper, and to Quesnel and Whistler on the west coast. In 1997 the company leased these eastbound GP40-3s from HELM leasing and 804 and 803 are seen crossing Ainslee Creek Trestle on the CN line, before plunging into the adjacent tunnel. One does not need to be suffering from vertigo to feel slightly dizzy looking over the road parapet.

Right: In the 'ATSF/BNSF in Arizona' section, Page 116 et seq, reference was made to the famous old Route 66 road. In the area covered in this short chapter between Barstow and Topock the route is rarely far away from the ATSF/BNSF main line. Dusk approaches at Barstow Yard on 28 March 1996 and SD39u No 1556 and its 'slug' No 1142 (converted from ATSF SD40-2 5208) are going about their hump yard switching business. A 'slug' comprises an old heavily ballasted locomotive frame mounted on powered trucks, with traction motors fed with 'surplus' electrical current from the generator of its parent locomotive. Barstow is a major junction combining the 1883/4 main line from Mojave to Barstow and Needles with the Cajon to San Bernardino and Los Angeles route. In addition to a major locomotive repair, maintenance and refuelling facility the yard has 48 classification tracks, 10 receiving tracks and 10 departure tracks. Out of a Barstow population of 21,000 nearly 1,000 are employed on the railroad.

Below: Excluding locomotive rebuilding and liveries this scene could have been recorded in 1966 rather than 1996. A delightful line-up of 'Geeps' is seen eastbound on an equally delightful mixed manifest at Fenner, California, in the Needles sub-division. With the vertical exhaust being commensurate with the power setting of the locomotives it is clear that this quartet are working hard as they climb towards Goffs with an eastbound freight. This lash-up includes ATSF GP35 2924 leads GP20u 3065 (ex-2046), GP30 2723 and GP20u 3049 (ex-2034). Of interest are the Clipper Mountains in the far right background, which are largely comprised of old volcanoes, the conductors on the conventional telegraph posts and the I-40 highway in the left background.

Right: Pure, unadulterated desert at Ludlow, California at 17.17 on 12 October 1998 and the piggybacks are on the move. The TOFC hot-shot is of considerable historical and chronological interest by virtue of its story telling locomotive livery variations. At the rear is Sante Fe Warbonnet GP60M 121, the last new locomotive being delivered in this colour scheme in September 1995. Following the merger the Warbonnet theme continued until 1997 but with the abbreviation 'BNSF' on the bodysides and cab front, all part of the 'superfleet' livery, as seen on lead Dash 9-44CW 779. The next stage was the introduction of Heritage 1 or 'Pumpkin' livery displayed by the second Dash 9 locomotive 1050. The third GE unit 4830 shows the Heritage 2 livery. There were to be two further major changes of livery before BNSF finally made their corporate mind up after changing their name to the 'BNSF Railway Company' in January 2005. In 2009 the 'Sage of Omaha', Warren Buffet, took a major $39bn shareholding in the company through his Berkshire Hathaway investment company, hoping for a good long term return on his investment.

.............and so we come to the end of our armchair photographic railtour of the 'Wild West'. The mountains, forests, deserts, plains and canyons of the American and Canadian west all contribute to a very rich railroad scene, suitably enhanced by remarkable trains, impressive locomotives, vibrant liveries, fantastic trestles, viaducts, bridges and tunnels, the various seasons of the year and remarkably diverse weather. It has been a pleasure to share these images with you and I hope you have enjoyed the experience. It is 17.53 on 13 October 1998 at Topock, east of

Needles, and the shutter is pressed to record the last train of the photographic day. Looking like solid 24 carat gold is this impressive double stack train, with a good old cowl unit thrown into the consist for good luck. Curving towards the Colorado River are BNSF B40-8 502, C44-9W 669, F45 5979 and C44-9W 743. Within two minutes the train will pass from California into Arizona and darkness will fall, ending yet another day in our lives.